LONDON.

n the Time of Queen Elizabeth.

Holywell Street, Strand, Jan.ry 1.st 1813.

Nigel Cawthorne has written more than 160 books under his own and several pen names. He claims to be the only man you will ever meet who has been in the dock of the Old Bailey and testified to the US Senate. The first was for a youthful indiscretion; the second was over a book that was not even published in America. He has a BSc (Hons) in physics from University College, London – making him one of the 'godless of Gower Street' – and fell into writing after supporting himself in his student years as a printers' messenger. This is an occupation now overtaken by ISDN lines and the Internet, but it taught him his way around the streets of London. A brief career in journalism on both sides of the Atlantic turned him into a writing machine and he now spends all hours, six days a week in the Reading Rooms of the British Library.

THE
LUDICROUS LAWS
OF
OLD LONDON

Nigel Cawthorne

ROBINSON

ROBINSON

First published in Great Britain in 2016 by Robinson

Text copyright © Nigel Cawthorne, 2016

The moral right of the author has been asserted.

A CIP catalogue record for this book
is available from the British Library.

ISBN: 978-1-47213-746-3

Typeset in Great Britain by Hewer Text UK Ltd, Edinburgh
Printed and bound in Great Britain by Clays Ltd, St Ives plc

Papers used by Robinson are from well-managed
forests and other responsible sources

MIX
Paper from
responsible sources
FSC® C104740
www.fsc.org

Robinson
An imprint of
Little, Brown Book Group
Carmelite House
50 Victoria Embankment
London EC4Y 0DZ

An Hachette UK Company
www.hachette.co.uk

www.littlebrown.co.uk

Contents

Introduction

THERE ARE PLENTY of ludicrous things about
London. For example, it has long been the largest
city in Europe – for some time it was the largest city
in the world – but its hinterland is a country, England,
that is somewhat smaller than New York State.

Much of London pretends not to be a city at all. It is
built around numerous parks and squares. That is because,
after the Restoration of the monarchy in 1660, when royal-
ists returned to London, which had been staunchly

1

parliamentarian during the Civil War and subsequent Commonwealth, they wanted to look out on greenery as if they were still living in the countryside.

There is also the curious matter of the City and the city. The City of London with a capital C means the square mile of the walled settlement first occupied by the Romans. The city, meaning the larger expanse of London, includes the City of Westminster, which was once a separate entity, a mile upriver from the other City, but has now merged into one conurbation.

To this day, the square mile is protected by its own City of London Police Force, which also has jurisdiction in two of the Inns of Court – the Middle and Inner Temples – where barristers reside. Then there are the dragons holding the shield of the City that appear as boundary markers on the thoroughfares into and out of it; beyond that, the Metropolitan Police hold sway.

Unlike other twin cities, Westminster and the City of London are not separated by a river. Both are on the north bank of the Thames; Southwark is on the south bank. Formerly in the county of Surrey, it has long since became part of London, which spread to incorporate and overwhelm other villages formerly in Surrey, Kent, Middlesex and Essex. The City remains the financial district, ruled over by the Lord Mayor of London, elected each year by the liverymen of the City's ancient trade associations and guilds; while the city is run by the Mayor, who is elected by the general populace in the metropolis and sits for four years. Guess which one has a golden coach.

There is also the crazy layout of the city. Most other modern cities have a logical design of broad avenues and straight streets, not unlike the gridiron plans of most North American cities. London had the opportunity to impose some order on the sprawl after the Great Fire of London in 1666 and the great architect of St Paul's cathedral, Sir Christopher Wren, drew up plans which he submitted to Charles II. However, although the buildings had been burnt down, individual freeholders still owned the land beneath the ashes and the razed areas had to be rebuilt along the lines of the old streets, which originally marked field boundaries.

Of course, London abounds with all manner of ludicrous laws that have been inherited in the same way. Laws have been made in London for over two thousand years and while legislators find it easy to make statutes, they often forget about repealing. When the Normans arrived in 1066, they tried to impose the 'Forest Law' that was widespread on the Continent. But gradually that fell into disuse and was replaced by what judges could remember of the earlier Saxon law. This became the basis of Common Law, which has been building up for over eight hundred years now. Despite the efforts of the Law Commission to cut out the deadwood, there are some medieval laws that are still in force.

The statutes of Common Law passed in Parliament are supplemented by case law made by decisions in a courtroom. Although there are assizes around the country, the higher courts sit in London. There were prize courts concerning war booty, chivalric courts, ecclesiastical courts, the Earl Marshal's court, the Court of the Exchequer and the Court of Chancery. Now there are principally the Central Criminal Court, known as the Old Bailey, the Royal Courts of Justice in the Strand and the Supreme Court that sits in Middlesex Guildhall in Parliament Square, Westminster. In 2009, this twelve-member court of last resort took over from the twelve Law Lords – more accurately the Lords of Appeal in Ordinary – who sat in the House of Lords.

Then there is the Privy Council – formally the monarch's closest advisors – whose Judicial Committee is the final court of appeal from British crown colonies and some members of the Commonwealth. Other county courts and magistrates' courts also sit in London.

The Inns of Court, which are home to barristers practising in England, Wales and, formerly, Ireland, are found in London, situated conveniently between the City and Westminster. They have their own bylaws, as does the City of London and its livery companies.

London has its own special status under the Magna Carta of 1215. Clause thirteen says: 'The city of London shall enjoy all its ancient liberties and free customs as well by land as by water . . .'

This is still in force. However, clause twelve says: 'No scutage or aid may be imposed in our kingdom unless by common counsel of our kingdom, except for the ransoming of our person, for making our eldest son a knight, and for once marrying our eldest daughter, and for these only a reasonable aid may be levied. Be it done in like manner concerning aids from the city of London.'

Scutage is the tax paid by vassal to his lord in lieu of military service, while aid is a levy or subsidy paid to the Crown to defray military and other extraordinary expenses. Although the laws in Magna Carta were supposed 'to be kept in our Kingdom of England forever', this is one of the sixty clauses that has been repealed. Only three remain enacted. I don't suppose this means that Londoners don't have to cough up when a prince is given some extra honour or a princess gets married.

However, under a charter granted by Henry I around 1131, Londoners are excused from trial by combat. Which is good to know.

Nigel Cawthorne

The Wonders of Westminster

While the laws of the land emanate from the Houses of Parliament in Westminster, the proceedings within are bound by some very ludicrous laws indeed. Some of these spring from the absurd anomaly that the other estates of the nation – one of which is elected – sit in what is technically a royal palace, though it ceased to be used as a royal residence in 1512.

DRESS CODE

Members of Parliament are forbidden from wearing armour in the House. Obviously this keeps honourable members who have spent all night at a drunken fancy-dress party from entering the chamber. But, actually, the law was passed in 1313 and was designed to stop men coming to Parliament armed or backed by force, so that debates could be carried on peaceably. The decree issued by Edward II says that 'in all Parliaments, Treatises and other Assemblies, which should be made in the Realm of England for ever, that every Man shall come without all Force and Armour'. This was a wise precaution.

The King was not popular at the time because of his relations with his favourite and probable lover Piers Gaveston, who had been seized by the barons and executed in 1312. Edward then took up with Hugh le Despenser. He was imprisoned by his queen, Isabella, and her lover Roger Mortimer, and died, it is said, by having a red-hot poker shoved up 'those parts in which he had been wont to take his vicious pleasure'. The law against wearing armour is still in force.

Swords may not be worn either. In the cloakroom, each MP has a loop of ribbon where such weapons could be left. These days, they usually hold umbrellas. No uniforms, decorations or military insignia are permitted either.

Hats are also forbidden, though traditionally a member would don a hat if he wanted to raise a point

8

of order during a division. Collapsible top hats were kept for the purpose until the rule was done away with in 1998.

No Eating or Drinking

Members may not eat or drink in the chamber. One exception to this is the Chancellor, who may have an alcoholic drink while delivering the Budget statement. In years gone by, the Speaker used to be able to adjourn proceedings in the House in order to have a meal. This was known as the 'Speaker's chop'. And long before smoking was outlawed in public buildings, it was banned in the chamber. However, members are allowed to take snuff and the doorkeeper keeps a snuffbox in case MPs feel the need.

Animals, except for guide dogs, are also banned.

No Reading, No Names

Speeches may not simply be read out during debate, although members are allowed to refer to notes. Similarly, the reading of newspapers, magazines and letters is not allowed. No visual aids, such as diagrams and maps, may be used in the chamber. The force of argument alone must be deployed, though a certain amount of booing, shouting, heckling and waving of order papers is allowed.

In the chamber, MPs must not use each other's names. If a member is of the same party, an MP must either refer to them as 'my honourable friend' or 'my right honourable friend' if the colleague is a member of the Privy Council. When referring to members from other parties, they are addressed as 'the honourable (or right honourable) lady or gentleman' or 'the honourable member for . . .' followed by the name of their constituency.

NO DYING

Although it is not technically against the law, no one is allowed to die in Parliament. If anyone has the misfortune to collapse with a fatal heart attack there, their body is removed before the death certificate is issued at St Thomas' which, being just the other side of Westminster Bridge, is the closest hospital. As the Palace of Westminster is a royal palace, anyone dying in a royal palace comes under the jurisdiction of the coroner of the royal household. However, if the coroner has to empanel a jury to investigate the death, all members of the jury have to be drawn from members of the royal household. This led to some controversy concerning the independence of the jury in the 2006 second inquest into the death of Diana, Princess of Wales. As a result the office of the royal coroner was abolished in 2013. No one has tested the water and attempted to discover what happens if you die in the Palace of Westminster since then.

On the upside, thanks to Parliament's status as a royal palace, the bars have always been open long after normal hours and have never been subject to the licensing laws. MPs could also play roulette or blackjack in the lobbies if they wished.

CLOTH OF ESTATE

The House of Lords Precedence Act of 1539 states: 'No person or persons of what estate degree or condition whatsoever he may be of, except only the King's children, shall at any time hereafter attempt to presume to sit or have place at any side of the cloth of estate in the parliament chamber, neither of the one hand of the King's Highness nor of the other, whether the King's Majesty be there personally present or absent.'

It seems that this law has been broken on numerous occasions by Prince Philip, the Duke of Edinburgh, who has, so far, escaped punishment.

It happens each time there is a state opening of Parliament. The Queen and Prince Philip ride to the Palace of Westminster in a carriage. Then in full regalia they process into the House of Lords. Members of the House of Commons are then summoned by an official called Black Rod and the Queen reads the 'Queen's Speech' which sets out the government's agenda for the coming session.

During previous reigns, when England had a king instead of a queen, the two thrones under the canopy in the House of Lords at the state opening were occupied by the King and the Prince of Wales or heir presumptive, while the Queen Consort sat to the left of the King on a chair slightly lower. However, when the Queen came to the throne, this third chair was removed and Prince Philip sat in the throne formerly occupied by the Prince of Wales. This follows a precedence set by Prince Albert, Queen Victoria's prince consort, who also seems to have been a habitual offender against Henry VIII's statute but is now beyond the reach of the law.

Plainly, neither Prince Albert nor Prince Philip are the child of the reigning monarch. But what exactly is the cloth of estate they are not supposed to sit next to? Officials of the House of Lords maintain that it is a carpet that covers the steps in front of the throne when the Queen is sitting on it and is usually kept rolled up under it. But according to the *Oxford English Dictionary*, the cloth of estate is 'a cloth spread over a throne or other seat of dignity; a canopy; a balda-chin' – which is a tent-like structure woven from silk and gold thread placed over a throne, not a carpet up to it. It ought to be pointed out that the current throne in the House of Lords has a carved wooden canopy. No matter. Whatever the cloth of estate was, Randolph Churchill maintained in the *Daily Telegraph* of 1 December 1952, the law no longer applied because it would have been destroyed in 1834 when the old Palace of Westminster burnt down.

The distinguished lawyer Edward F. Iwi took issue with this. He maintained that the original canopy mentioned in the 1539 Act would have worn out long before 1834 and there would have been several cloths of estate in the meantime. That did not mean the law was invalid.

He pointed to the Statute Law Revision Act of 1948, which amended section two of the House of Lords Precedence Act of 1539, but left section one, which mentions the cloth of estate, alone. If the cloth of estate no longer existed, he argued, surely Parliament would have repealed it.

'The failure to repeal section one shows that the legislature believed that the existing canopy over the throne is the cloth of estate,' he reasoned.

He also pointed to the Standing Orders of the House of Lords, adopted on 27 March 1621, which say: 'When the House is sitting, every Lord is to make obeisance to the cloth of estate on entering the House.'

These Standing Orders are still in force and lords are still required to bow towards the throne upon entering the chamber. But what they are bowing to is the cloth of estate as there is no obligation to bow to the throne. So even if the original piece of cloth from the sixteenth century was long gone, in law, it still exists, so Prince Philip is a persistent lawbreaker.

However, the 1539 Act fails to specify what the penalties were for breaking this provision. It seems that sitting alongside the cloth of estate was so heinous a crime that whoever framed the law could not imagine anyone having the temerity to commit it. To break this law was just unthinkable – just as it was not necessary to specify a punishment for breaking the law of gravity.

Again Edward F. Iwi comes to our aid. He pointed out that the Diplomatic Privileges Act of 1708 likewise specifies no tariff. Just how heinous a crime that Act seeks to prohibit is spelt out in its preamble: 'Whereas several turbulent and disorderly persons having in a most outrageous manner insulted the person of his excellency Andrew Artemonowitz Mattueof, ambassador extraordinary of his Czarist Majesty, Emperor of Great Russia, Her Majesty's good friend and ally, by arresting him, and taking him by violence out of his coach in the public street, and detaining him in custody for several hours, in contempt of the protection granted by Her Majesty, contrary to the law of nations, and in prejudice of the rights and privileges which ambassadors and other public ministers, authorised and received as such, have at all times been thereby possessed of, and ought to be kept sacred and inviolable . . .'

Section four which deals with penalties and simply says that the 'violators of the law of nations and disturbers of the public repose . . . shall suffer such pains, penalties and corporal punishment as the lord chancellor, lord keeper and chief justices, or any two of them, shall judge fit to be imposed and inflicted'. According to Edward Iwi, it sounds like the Duke of Edinburgh is long overdue for a sound thrashing.

14

ALIVE OR DEAD?

During the Second World War an effort was made to amend the Deputy Speaker Act of 1855. Until this Act, the House of Commons could not sit if the speaker was indisposed. If he died, a new speaker must be elected and, by custom, taken forcibly to the chair, but if he was unwell or otherwise unable to attend Parliament the sitting was suspended.

Under the Deputy Speaker Act of 1855 though, if the speaker was not present for whatever reason, the chairman of the House ways and means committee could sit in his place as deputy speaker, with all the procedural powers of the speaker himself. But wartime brought with it a problem. What would happen if the place where the speaker was taking shelter was hit by a bomb and it could not be ascertained, possibly for days, whether the speaker was alive or dead? Could the deputy speaker continue in his stead, or would the sitting have to be suspended?

This was a matter of some concern because, during wartime, Acts were being rushed through Parliament and given royal assent within a matter of hours. Imagine that there had been an air raid, the deputy speaker assumed that the speaker had survived, a bill passed both Houses and received royal assent – and then it turned out that the speaker was dead. In that case, the Act would be invalid.

As the war was being fought against tyranny for democracy and the rule of law, this was of some importance. An amendment was drafted in 1941, but no parliamentary time could be found to lay it before the House. Then, early in 1943, the speaker fell ill and the urgency of passing the bill became all too clear. It was scheduled for 3 March 1943, along with a debate on the navy estimates. But that very day the speaker died and the deputy speaker was forced to suspend the sitting. In fact, the House was adjourned until the following Tuesday and the House was out of action for five whole days during wartime. It was only then that a new speaker was elected and the navy estimates could be debated.

RETURNING DEFEATED

Under UK law it was possible for a government that had lost an election to return to government, even though it had been thrashed at the polls. This was a consequence of the Meeting of Parliament Act of 1797, which was designed to tie the hands of the sovereign, preventing them from recalling a parliament that they had dissolved or changing the date of a general election. One unfortunate consequence of this is that, if a national emergency arose after Parliament had been dissolved, Parliament could not meet again to deal with the crisis until after the general election had taken place at the date already fixed.

However, if the monarch died during this period, the old Parliament was automatically recalled and continued to sit for another six months. This occurred even if polling had taken place and the current occupants of the government benches had been voted out. The situation was only rectified by the Representation of the People's Act in 1985, nearly 200 years after the law causing the problem was first enacted.

STRICT ATTENDANCE

It was only in 1993 that the 1514 Attendance in Parliament Act was repealed. This required that no one 'elected to come or be in parliament . . . depart from the said parliament, nor absent himself from the same, till parliament be fully ended or prorogued . . . upon pain of . . . losing all those sums of money which he or they should or ought to have had for his or their wages'. That would keep them from attending board meetings or enjoying a boozy lunch at one of their clubs.

An even older law of 1382, which is still in force, demands that both members of the House of Lords and House of Commons turn up when called. It was called, snappily, 'Every one to whom it belongeth, shall upon summons come to the parliament'. Under it anyone absent without a reasonable or honest excuse 'shall be amerced [fined] or otherwise punished in the manner as was accustomed to be done in the said case in times passed'. So if they are making a quick buck in the city or dallying with their mistresses, MPs face a stiff fine as well as a loss of wages.

LAWYERS EXCLUDED FROM PARLIAMENT

Lawyers have been disqualified from sitting as members of the House of Commons in Westminster. Indeed, they were the first class of person positively excluded from the House, according to a writ in the time of Edward III (1327–77), which said that the Commons should be *gladiis cinctos* – girded with swords. Beforehand, lawyers abounded in the House because for just four shillings a day it was not worth a knight of the shire going to the trouble and inconvenience of moving to London, while lawyers were already there because the law courts sat at the same times as Parliament. To exclude them all the more effectually, it was declared that, if elected, they should not receive the wages paid to the members in those days. A summons issued in the fifth year of Henry IV (1399–1413) says: 'The King willed that neither you, nor any other sheriff (vicecomes) of the kingdom, or any apprentice, nor other man following the law should be chosen.'

It was said that this prohibition led to the *indoctum parliamentum*, or lack-learning Parliament. After that, lawyers were returned, though the Puritan William Prynne (1600–69) argued that keeping lawyers out of the House of Commons shortened the duration of the session, facilitated the despatch of business and had the desirable effect of 'restoring laws to their primitive Saxon simplicity, and making them most like God's commandments'. A further attempt was made to remove lawyers during the Commonwealth. Sadly, these days,

Parliament and the government are packed with lawyers once again. And they are being paid.

STAYING AWAKE

In the reign of George III a bill was introduced to the House of Commons for the improvement of the metropolitan watch. One of its clauses stipulated that watchmen were to be compelled to sleep during the day. When it was heard in committee, a baronet stood up and asked that this provision be extended to Members of Parliament. He had been suffering from gout. The discomfort had robbed him of sleep for many nights and he said he would be glad to come under the operations of the enactment.

GREENWICH VILLAGE

When the American revolutionaries were demanding 'no taxation without representation', the matter was debated in the House of Commons, where Sir James Marriott bravely maintained that the American colonies were indeed represented in Parliament.

'Although it has been frequently pretended that the inhabitants of the colonies are not represented in the British Parliament, yet the fact is otherwise, for they are actually represented,' he said. 'The first colonisation was by sovereign authority in Virginia, and the grants of those lands were expressed in a royal charter, "to have and to hold of the King's majesty, as part and parcel of the manor of East Greenwich . . . ".'

The inhabitants of the United States would be no doubt delighted to discover that they are represented in Parliament by the MP for the Greater London constituency of Greenwich and Woolwich, currently Matthew Pennycook, Labour. Unfortunately, at the time, this discovery was greeted by laughter in the House, while on the other side of the Atlantic the truculent Americans went to war.

Toffs on Trial

Under English Common Law it is your right to be tried by your peers. This is guaranteed by clause thirty-nine of the Magna Carta signed at Runnymede in 1215, or clause twenty-nine of the 1297 version. That meant, until the passing of the 1948 Criminal Justice Act, clause 30, members of the House of Lords had the right to be tried by the House, if it was sitting. If Parliament was in recess, the hearing would take place in the Court of the High Steward, with only the law lords present.

Even in 1935, this only applied in cases of treason or a felony. Other crimes were tried before ordinary courts. In December that year, Edward Southwell Russell, twenty-sixth Baron de Clifford, insisted on his right to be tried before the House of Peers for the manslaughter of Douglas George Hopkins, who had been killed in a car accident on the Kingston bypass in August that year. This was the last trial to take place before the lords spiritual and temporal, peers of the realm, the archbishops and bishops, and the judges.

The peers were marshalled in the Palace of Westminster's royal gallery – a huge room 40 ft wide and 140 ft long – by the Norroy Kings of Arms, Chief Herald North of the Trent, while the defendant was in the custody of the Gentleman Usher of Black Rod. Presiding was the Lord Chancellor, the Lord High Steward, who sat before the throne. The Norroy and Black Rod approached the Lord High Steward, bowing low three times on the way, and presented him with his symbol of office, the White Staff. The trial then got under way.

After hearing the prosecution and the defence, the peers and judges filed out, and the Lord High Steward asked each of them in turn, starting with the most junior, whether they found the defendant 'guilty or not guilty'. Each had to reply either 'guilty upon my honour' or 'not guilty upon my honour'. As it was they unanimously found de Clifford not guilty.

BIGAMY

Before peers lost the right to be tried before the House of Lords, a woman could be married to two men and not be found guilty of bigamy – if the first marriage was to a commoner and the second to a peer of the realm. As a peeress, she would have had the right to be tried by the House of Lords, who would have been obliged to acquit her. If they had tried to convict, they would have established the first marriage in law, which would mean that she was not a peeress and they would have no jurisdiction. Equally, if a crown court tried to convict, it would acknowledge the rank conferred by her second marriage, negating its own jurisdiction.

LORDS AND LADIES

Over the years, the composition of the House of Lords has changed constantly. In 2004 their Lordships were discussing the Gender Recognition bill, which allows transvestites and transsexuals to be recognised in law under their assumed or acquired gender. While considering the bill, they were forced to consider some aspects that applied only to those entitled to the coronet and ermine. For example, would an Earl who changed gender become a Countess? In fact, it was discovered that they would have to apply to the monarch to have their title changed.

Another point still was brought up by Earl Ferrers: he asked the House to consider if an earl sired a daughter followed by a son. The son, being the Earl's oldest son, would be his heir and would be styled, by courtesy, viscount, while the daughter would be plain old 'Lady'. But say the lady experiences what the bill calls 'gender dysphoria', dresses up as a man and lives as a man for two years, or even undergoes gender-reassignment surgery. Now, with a doctor's note, he can appear before the local Gender Recognition Panel that the subsequent Act set up. They can then give him a certificate saying that he is a man and has hence become the oldest son of an Earl. What Earl Ferrers wanted to know was could he now style himself viscount? Would the younger brother lose his right to the title? And when the Earl died, would the transgendered viscount succeed to earldom? There might even be a stately home and country estate that went along with the title. The noble Lord Ferrers received no clear answer.

HABEAS CORPUS

There is no mention of *habeas corpus* – that cornerstone of liberty – in the Magna Carta. That did not enter statute until 464 years later with the *Habeas Corpus* Act of 1679. Even then it is not sure that it was passed legally by both Houses of Parliament. The Act came about because a London lady liked a drink or two. One night in 1621, Alice Robinson and her husband were holding a rowdy, drunken party at their home in High Holborn. A passing constable heard 'a brawling, fighting noise' and entered the house to investigate. Inside, he said, he found 'men and women in disordered and uncivil accompanying together'. Sounds fun. The party-pooping policeman accused Alice of keeping the whole parish awake with her revelry. She swore at him. He arrested her and she was banged up in the Clerkenwell House of Correction on Bowling Green Lane, EC1.

Apparently Alice's fellow revellers missed her wild parties and pushed for her release. Eventually they forced the authorities to bring her before the courts. At the Old Bailey she told a harrowing tale. She said that, at the Clerkenwell House of Correction, she had been stripped and given fifty lashes.

'I swooned,' she said, 'my flesh being torn by the whips.'

She had been forced to sleep on the bare earth and fed nothing but water and black bread. This was harsh even by the standards of the time. Then it came out that she was pregnant. There was an outcry. The jury acquitted her and the constable who had nicked her found himself in Newgate Prison on the grounds that he had arrested her without a warrant. The Justice of the Peace who had signed the warrant for her detention was also reprimanded.

The result was the *Habeas Corpus* Act which takes its name from the first words of the writ issued to enforce it: '*Habeas corpus ad subjiciendum* . . .' which means 'You should have the body for submitting . . .' Once the writ has been presented a gaoler had to produce the prisoner, or their corpse, within three days. It means that the authorities cannot hold a person for an unreasonable amount of time before releasing them or bringing them before a court and is the rock that individual liberty is built on throughout the common-law countries.

However, it took some time after Alice's release for the *Habeas Corpus* Act to reach the statute books as there was the small matter of the Civil War to get over with first. In fact, the Act may not be a law at all as it was not actually approved by both Houses of Parliament. After the Restoration, the *Habeas Corpus* bill had to be introduced several times. Each time it romped through the Commons but met stiff opposition in the House of Lords. Eventually it was passed by a disgraceful piece of chicanery. According to the Bishop of Salisbury, Gilbert Burnet, on the third reading, 'Lords Grey and Norris were named to be tellers. Lord Norris, being a man subject to the vapours, was not at all times attentive to what he was doing. So a very fat lord coming in, Lord Grey counted him for ten, as a jest a first; but seeing Lord Norris had not observed it, he went on with his misreckoning of ten; so was it reported to the House, and declared that they who were for the bill were the majority, though it indeed went on the other side.'

Certainly there had been some jiggery-pokery. The vote in the House of Lords was recorded at fifty-seven to fifty-five, though the minute book of the Lords says that there were only 107 peers present. Realising that something was amiss, Lord Chancellor Shaftesbury, a fervent supporter of the bill, got to his feet and talked for nearly an hour on all sorts of other matters. During that time a number of peers entered and left the House, so it was impossible to have a recount. Parliament was reaching the end of its session so, without any further ado, the bill received royal assent.

25

WESTMINSTER HALL

Until the reign of Edward III, all the courts used to follow the King as he travelled around the country. Indeed a law passed by Edward I in 1309 insisted that the Lord Chancellor and King's Bench follow him where he went, so if you wanted to get a judgement in a case you were constantly on the move.

But with the beginnings of the Hundred Years War, Edward III wanted to spend more time in France, so the King's Bench and the Court of the Chancery settled in Westminster Hall. Built in 1097, it is now the oldest part of the Palace of Westminster. The two courts sat in the open hall – which must have caused some confusion – with the King's Bench occupying the left-hand side of the room and the Chancery the right-hand side, with a bar to keep the crowd back, preventing them from swamping the judge. The Chancellor, 'on account of his superior dignity', sat on a marble chair on a raised platform.

To add to the confusion, there were also shops in the hall that did brisk business during the hearings. They continued doing business there until 1630 when, on Saturday night, a woman left a pan of hot coals under one of the stalls and the shops caught on fire. The hall itself was only saved when two sailors climbed up on the roof, opened the lead and poured water down on the flames. After that Charles I ordered that there should be no more shopping done in his courtrooms.

A Duchess or a Countess

Charles I was tried in Westminster Hall. Other notable defendants that appeared there include William Wallace, Thomas More and Guy Fawkes. But none attracted a more distinguished audience than that of a comely woman in her mid-fifties in 1776. The Queen and the Prince of Wales were there, attended by a detachment of the guards. Tickets changed hands at £20 a piece and part of the public stand collapsed, crushing one man's head. The trial was also notable because many of the jury – the peers ushered through from the adjoining House of Lords – had slept with the defendant.

In a private room in the palace she was bled by a doctor to lower her blood pressure. She was dressed demurely in widow's weeds, and when she entered the hall she was attended by a clergyman, three doctors and four ladies in waiting. Her trial was for bigamy. What the peers had to decide was whether she was a duchess or a countess, so the Lord High Steward addressed her only as madam.

Born Elizabeth Chudleigh around 1720, she was the daughter of Colonel Thomas Chudleigh, Lieutenant Governor of the Chelsea Hospital, who lost his money in the South Sea Bubble and died in 1726. She was brought up by her mother in Devon and when she was just fifteen, she was out walking one day when she was accosted by a middle-aged gentleman with a gun.

'Madam,' he said. 'He is a fortunate hunter who can come out of a wood and meet a divinity.'

27

In the simple manner of the age, she did what was expected of her.

The man was wealthy Whig politician William Pulteney, later first Earl of Bath and a member of the Privy Council. As a result of her endeavours, she became maid-of-honours to the Princess of Wales at a salary of £400 per annum – worth over £35,000 today. She took advantage of that position to make herself available to any man of sufficient wealth or social standing, including a large number of peers.

In 1743, the nineteen-year-old Duke of Hamilton – described by Robert Walpole as 'hot, debauched and extravagant' – proposed marriage. To thwart this, his family paid for her to go on the Grand Tour.

The following year she secretly married twenty-year-old John Hervey at eleven o'clock at night on 4 August 1744 in the parish church in Lainston near Salisbury, when she had been staying at her aunt's house nearby. They stayed together for three days before he returned to sea. Although he was the son of Baron Hervey of Ickworth and grandson of the first Earl of Bristol, he was a penniless naval lieutenant. During his brief shore leaves, she conceived and then had a child, which died.

Hervey did not have the money to support a wife. Others could and she eagerly advertised for patrons. At a masque in Somerset House to celebrate the defeat of the Young Pretender, she came as Iphigenia, stripped for sacrifice with a little greenery around her waist – 'so naked', wrote Mrs Montague, 'that the high priest could very easily inspect the entrails of the victim'.

The Princess of Wales threw a shawl over her. Infatuated George II asked if he could place his hand on her bare breasts. With great presence of mind, she offered to put it on a still softer place – and guided it to the royal forehead. Far from taking offence, the King gave her a thirty-five-guinea watch and made her mother a housekeeper at Windsor.

What went on between George and Elizabeth has not been vouchsafed to history. However her tactics secured her a new lover – Evelyn Pierrepont, second Duke of Kingston upon Hull – who kept her in the condition she had long sought. However, as she approached forty, she yearned for respectability – that is, money and a title.

A tantalising prospect beckoned when John Hervey's elder brother George, then Earl of Bristol, fell ill. If he died, John would inherit the title. Elizabeth dashed down to Hampshire and got the ailing priest who had married them to record the marriage in the parish register. She returned to London triumphant with her marriage lines recorded in the priest's own hand. Then disaster struck: George recovered.

Elizabeth resumed her duties as the smartest kept woman in London, giving lavish parties and socialising with the grandest in the land. Hervey now sought to marry another. But, in those days, it was only possible to obtain a divorce by a special Act of Parliament. This could only be done on the grounds of adultery. Elizabeth was unwilling to publicly declare that she was an adulteress, so she cooked up another plan.

She would bring an action in the Ecclesiastical Court, which had jurisdiction of the matters relating to the sacraments, including marriage, for jactitation – that is, boasting erroneously that he was her husband. She is said to have paid him £16,000 to counter-sue, insisting that he was indeed her husband, but making a lame case. It worked. In February 1769 the court found in her favour, ruling that the marriage had not taken place. On 8 March Elizabeth married the Duke of Kingston at St George's, Hanover Square.

Three years later, he died, leaving his entire estate to her, provided she did not marry again. His nephew and former heir Evelyn Medows disputed the will, alleging that her marriage to his uncle was not legitimate and that she was a bigamist as her divorce had been obtained dishonestly.

While Medows marshalled his case, Elizabeth travelled widely on the continent, ingratiating herself with Pope Clement XIV. George Hervey died and John became Earl of Bristol. So if her marriage to Pierrepont was not valid and she was still married to Hervey, she was a countess rather than a duchess.

The Lord Chief Justice, Lord Mansfield, was reluctant to bring the case before the House of Lords until the principle of *cui bono* – who befits – saying: 'The lady makes you a curtsy and you return a bow.' But the public was not to be cheated of such a juicy spectacle.

Nor was Elizabeth. Rather that risk being outlawed in her absence, she prepared to return to London. But her banker in Rome, fearing that the money on deposit did not belong to her, refused to hand it over, but changed his mind when she appeared with a pair of loaded pistols.

In Westminster Hall, Elizabeth went through all the proprieties of curtseying and kneeling, and entered a plea of not guilty. But one of her aunt's maidservants said that she had been present at the marriage and had seen the couple in bed together. And she testified that Elizabeth had had a child. The doctor who had delivered that child said Elizabeth had told him of her marriage. A number of peers, who had plainly slept with her, were also called, but refused to divulge the content of private conversion – clearly a stance at odds with the oath they had sworn 'to tell the truth, the whole truth, and nothing but the truth'.

The House had to adjourn to discuss the matter and concluded, inevitably under English law, that witnesses had no such privilege and had to answer all such questions. Their lordship who had been called then suffered from a communal attack of amnesia.

In her own defence, Elizabeth claimed that her marriage to Hervey had been such a scrambling and shabby affair as to amount to no marriage at all, while she had taken legal advice before marrying Pierrepont and had no intent to deceive anyone.

The peers returned a unanimous verdict of guilty, though the Duke of Newcastle, a neighbour and former lover, declared that she was 'guilty erroneously, not intentionally'.

The punishment for bigamy at the time was branding on the hand. She was spared this as she was still a peeress. While her coach headed back to her Knightsbridge house with one black-clad veiled occupant, Elizabeth herself raced to Dover. Once safely in France with her cash, she never returned.

In Munich, the elector created her Countess of Warth. In Vienna, the Pope asked Empress Maria Theresa to receive her as a duchess. In St Petersburg she was warmly welcomed by Catherine the Great, who gave her a mansion where she set up a vodka distillery, which she left to a young English carpenter, no doubt for services rendered.

She was wooed by the wealthy Prince Karl Stanislaw Radziwill, who strove to ply her with lavish gifts and showy spectacles. After a particularly expensive fireworks display, she remarked, 'He may fire as much as he pleases, but he shall not hit my mark.' Instead, she became involved with a mysterious stranger named Worta, who claimed to be an Albanian prince with the highest connections and played on her thirst for flattery. Having wheedled large sums of money out of her, he was unmasked as a swindler and arrested for forgery in Holland, where he committed suicide by taking poison.

In France she purchased a mansion at Montmartre, and a 300-bedroomed estate at St Assise, just outside Paris, for £50,000 from the Comte de Provence, later Louis XVIII. A civil suit arose over the Montmartre house; on hearing that she had lost the case, she threw such an hysterical tantrum that she burst an internal blood vessel. On the following day, 26 August 1788, she died suddenly in Paris. In her will she made generous provision for her nephews and their children, and was buried in Pierrepont, the ancestral village of the dukes of Kingston in the Île-de-France, making a point about her marriage to the Duke to the last.

Ludicrous Liveries

One of the oldest surviving traditions is the granting of the freedom of the City of London. It is thought that this was first done in 1237. In medieval times a freeman was someone who was not the property of a feudal lord and had the right to own land and earn money.

From 1390, the freedom of the City was bestowed by the livery companies. These

were established guilds and fraternities
that paid a large sum of money to the
Crown for a royal charter. The charter
gave the company legal incorporation,
the power to hold assemblies, and to
elect officers to rule the company and
carry out rights of search and to hold
land of a specified annual in perpetuity.
Within the larger companies, the senior
members of the company distinguished
themselves from ordinary members by
wearing the company livery. These
liverymen still elect the Lord Mayor.

FREEMEN OF THE CITY OF LONDON

The charter of their town or city granted freedom to
the tradesmen that lived within its walls, so craftsmen
coming to the city were issued a document making them
freemen. It would be conferred in a casket which a
freeman would carry around with him to prove he had
the right to work. Until 1835, anyone who carried on a
trade in the City had to be a freeman and a member of
one of the ancient guilds or livery companies. Since then
freedom of the city has been widened to incorporate not
just members of livery companies, but also people living
or working in the City, or those who had a strong London
connection. In 1908 a Guild of Freemen was formed as
an association for freemen who did not belong to any

City company. The guild still holds an annual banquet in the Guildhall.

There are a number of ancient privileges that come with being a freeman. Freemen have the right to herd sheep over London Bridge without being charged a toll, to go about the City with a drawn sword and, if convicted of a capital offence, to be hanged with a silken cord rather than the standard hemp rope. These rights are more of a collective memory than written law. Others are said to have included immunity from press-ganging, the right to marry in St Paul's Cathedral – though I imagine that this would be costly – the right to be buried within the City walls, and the right to be drunk and disorderly without fear of arrest. It is also thought that freemen are allowed to drive geese down Cheapside, though no one had tried this recently. These days it would contravene numerous traffic, animal health, food hygiene, and health and safety regulations. However, freemen have occasionally been allowed to exercise their right to drive sheep across London Bridge on a Sunday for charity.

While today the freedom of the City has no real privileges, it is still taken up by some 1,800 people every year. Before 1996, it was only open to British subjects or Commonwealth citizens over twenty-one years old and of good character. Now people of any nationality may apply. There is a long tradition of granting women the freedom of the City; they become 'free sisters'.

The livery companies have long since given up their original purposes and now operate as charitable trusts.

BARBERS AND SURGEONS

A law passed in 1540 – and still in force today – makes it illegal for barbers in the City of London to practise surgery. With impeccable impartiality, the Act also forbids surgeons to cut hair. The purpose of the Act, strangely, was to join the Company of Barbers and the Guild of Surgeons together in one livery company. However, as there was no separate guild for teeth-pullers, both barbers and surgeons were still allowed to work as dentists as the statute allows the 'drawing of teeth'.

Most barbers had been wielding a scalpel as well as a comb and scissors since 1163, when Pope Alexander III banned members of religious orders from shedding blood. As bleeding was used as a treatment for almost everything back then, this took the clergy out of medicine completely. Being equipped with a razor, the barbers took over.

The barbers of the City of London had got themselves organised early on, when in 1308 Richard le Barber was elected master of the Barbers' Guild. He was instructed by the Lord Mayor and aldermen to go round all the barbers every month and if he found any brothel keepers 'or other disreputable folk to the scandal of the craft' he was to arrest them and 'cause them to be brought before the chamber'.

Records show that the first surgeons joined the Barbers' Guild in 1312. It was an uneasy alliance and the surgeons applied for a licence to form the Guild of

Surgeons in 1368. But eight years later in 1376, the Lord Mayor and the aldermen allowed the Barbers' Guild to exercise supervision over the surgeons, who now concerned themselves with more serious work than mere bleeding. This began a power struggle between the two guilds. In 1462, the barbers won out when Edward IV granted them a Charter of Incorporation, giving their position in the City the royal seal.

The relationship between the Company of Barbers and the Guild of Surgeons continued to be strained due to demarcation problems. But in 1493 they thrashed out a set of rules for the practice of surgery in the City. Each selected two masters – one to control surgery, the other to handle hairdressing. They were allowed to fine anyone breaking the rules and, in more serious and persistent cases, could refer them to the Lord Mayor and aldermen for judgement.

In 1497 the Company and the Guild got together to grant what appears to be the earliest English diploma in surgery. But the barbers continued to have the upper hand and successive monarchs confirmed their Barbers' Charter. But in 1511, an Act of Parliament was passed which put the licensing of physicians and surgeons in the hands of the local bishop. So in the City, the Bishop of London took over supervision of the medical profession. Parliament also laid down that guilds and livery companies should have their ordinances approved by the legal profession, and in 1530 new rules for barbers and surgeons were agreed by the Lord Chancellor, Sir Thomas More. This document is still held by the

Worshipful Company of Barbers at Barber-Surgeons' Hall.

Ten years later, Henry VIII's surgeon Thomas Vicary urged the King to introduce proper regulation of the surgeons in the City. Consequently, the Surgeons Guild and the Company of Barbers were amalgamated by an Act of Parliament, forming the Company of Barber-Surgeons. The writ of the company lay within a radius of one mile from the City and Westminster.

The Act also allowed the united company to have the bodies of four executed criminals a year to be anatomised in public demonstrations. Charles II increased the annual cull to six. Presumably, the barbers could also cut the corpses' hair. The teaching of anatomy became an important function of the company and Inigo Jones designed an anatomy theatre for the company in 1636. The company also undertook the examination of surgeons for the navy.

Although the barbers and surgeons were in the same company they were not permitted to undertake each other's work. At this time the Barber-Surgeons had the largest number of freemen of any City livery company.

By 1745, surgeons outnumbered barbers in the City. They were developing new skills and felt they had little in common with humble hairdressers. They petitioned the House of Commons and the bill separating London's surgeons and barbers received the royal assent on 2 May 1745. The barbers retained the Barber-Surgeons' Hall, its silver and most of its treasures, while the surgeons departed to form first the Company of

Surgeons and later, in 1800, the Royal College of Surgeons.

Both the Barbers and Chirurgians Act of 1540 and the London Barbers and Surgeons Act of 1745 – with the exception of sections 12 and 15–18 – were repealed in 1986. Those unrepealed sections include the ones that prevent barbers from operating as surgeons and surgeons from cutting hair.

The Barbers' Hall was destroyed in the Great Fire of London 1666, rebuilt, and destroyed again by bombs in 1940. A new Barber-Surgeons' Hall in Monkwell Square, alongside the old London Wall, was opened in 1969.

FLETCHERS

The Worshipful Company of Fletchers was set up in the City of London in 1371, when the arrow-makers presented a petition to the Lord Mayor to make their trade separate and distinct from that of the bowyer, or bow-maker. Anyone caught working in both trades was fined £4. In 1385 the first masters and wardens of the company were sworn in and the company's first ordinances were issued on 16 June 1403.

In 1423 fletchers were forbidden to open their shops on Sundays and 'high feast days'. And in 1471 a law was passed that allowed the authorities to order fletchers, bowyers, stringers and arrowhead-makers who were not freemen of the City of London to move to other cities, boroughs or towns where there were no arrowhead or bow-makers 'for the maintenance of artillery and archery'. Even so there was such a shortage of bows and arrows in the kingdom that an Act had to be passed to allow them to be imported. It was illegal to admit women to the guilds but, in the sixteenth century, the fletchers allowed widows to join on the death of their husbands. Eventually even single women were allowed. Even so, the company informed a commission in 1887 that 'no women have hitherto been admitted'.

Although the fletchers are one of the oldest companies, they have one of the newest halls in Cloth Street, EC1. Built in the 1980s, it is shared with the Worshipful Company of Farmers.

APOTHECARIES

The Apothecaries Act of 1815 gave the City of London's Worshipful Society of Apothecaries the statutory right to conduct examinations and grant licences to practise medicine throughout England and Wales. It continues to license doctors to this day as a member of the United Examining Board, the only non-university medical licensing board in the UK.

Not only is it non-medical, the apothecaries used to be plain old grocers. They started off as the Guild of Pepperers, formed in the City in 1180. By 1316, the pepperers had been joined by the spicers. Later, they became wholesalers, dealing with goods *en gros* (meaning 'in bulk') – hence grocers – and incorporated as the Worshipful Company of Grocers in 1428. Although members continued to work in the growing spice trade, by the mid-sixteenth century specialist apothecaries had become the equivalent of today's high-street chemists. This brought them into conflict with the College of Physicians, which regulated medicine.

For many years London apothecaries who specialised in pharmacy petitioned to secede from the Grocers' Company. Their leader Gideon de Laune, a wealthy and influential Huguenot, was also apothecary to Anne of Denmark, wife of James I of England, who signed the royal charter incorporating the Worshipful Society of Apothecaries on 6 December 1617.

King James explained his decision to the House of Commons in 1624: 'I myself did devise that corporation and do allow it. The grocers who complain of it are but merchants; the mystery of these apothecaries belonging to apothecaries, wherein the grocers are unskilful; and therefore I think it is fitting they should be a corporation of themselves.'

In 1632, the society acquired the guesthouse of the Dominican Priory of Blackfriars as their livery hall. It was destroyed in the Great Fire of London, but rebuilt on the same site in 1672 and is still standing today. Until 1922, the Society of Apothecaries manufactured and sold medical and pharmaceutical products at the hall. It also ran the Chelsea Physic Garden, founded in 1673, only relinquishing control in 1899.

In 1704, the society won a key legal suit against the Royal College of Physicians, known as the 'Rose case'. In February 1701, an apothecary named Rose had sent 'boluses, electuaries and juleps' – large round pills, syrups and medicated drinks – to a man named Seale. Rose was prosecuted for 'practising physic' without a licence, in contravention of an Act of Henry VIII, who had granted a charter to the College of Physicians in 1518. He was convicted and appealed. The case went to the House of Lords, which ruled that apothecaries could both dispense and prescribe medicine. The college tried to strike back several times, but bills attempting to reassert their monopoly on doctoring failed. Finally, the Apothecaries Act regulating the situation was passed in 1815. It allowed apothecaries to practise after five years' training. As a consequence, apothecaries evolved into today's general practitioners. So next time you visit the doctor, don't forget to ask for some pepper and spices as well.

GARBLING SPICES

In 1604, James I permitted the 'garbling of spices' in the City of London. Indeed the City of London Garbling of Spices and Admission of Brokers Act authorised the Lord Mayor and aldermen to appoint an official garbler whose duties were 'at the request of any person or persons, owner or owners of any spices, drugs or other wares or merchandises garbleable, and not otherwise,

[to] garble the same'. The Act repealed the 1604 Act for the Well Garbling of Spices.

'To garble', in this sense, means to remove impurities by sifting. The 1604 Act was repealed in 1707. However, clause fourteen of the City of London Elections Act of 1724, which is still in force, allows the City to appoint, rather than elect, the 'coroner, common crier, commissioners of sewer and garbler'.

BAKERS

The Bakers' Guild had the task of enforcing the Assize of Bread and Ale within two miles of the City of London, excluding the City of Westminster. The assize was maintained by the Court or Halimot of Holy-Moot – 'moot' is an old word for a court – which sat in the guild's hall with a jury formed of the wardens and aldermen, and a pair of scales to detect short weights. It also kept an eye out for bakers who put sand in the flour – a common practice to judge from the teeth of the people of the time. Sawdust was also added.

The penalty for a serious offence was to be dragged through the dirtiest streets of the City on a hurdle with an offending loaf hung around the neck. A second offence would earn an hour in the pillory. If convicted a third time, a baker would have his oven demolished and be forced to forswear baking. They would certainly not be able to continue in business in the City, as the Worshipful Company of Bakers' issued annual hallmarks – similar to those used on precious metal – for certified bakers to mark their loaves.

Bakers were so fearful of giving short weight that they would give a small extra piece of bread with each loaf. With an order of twelve loaves, they would give one loaf free, hence the 'bakers' dozen.

In the fourth century, the Brown-Bakers' Guild, which made loaves using rye, barley or buckwheat, split the White-Bakers' Guild. The Brown-Bakers were bakers of nutritious brown bread, while the White-Bakers were bakers of the less nutritious but more popular white bread. The White-Bakers were incorporated by a royal charter of 1509, while the Brown-Bakers were incorporated in 1621. But in 1645, due to a decline in trade, they were forced to reunite. The Worshipful Company of Bakers got a new charter in 1686.

The Assizes of Bread and Ale ended in 1815. After that the weight of a standard loaf was fixed by statute.

Harp Lane, Billingsgate, has been the site of Bakers' Hall since 1506. It once contained a courtroom where trade-related misdemeanours were tried and the present hall dates from 1964 after the previous building was destroyed in the Second World War.

FISHMONGERS

Until the end of the fourteenth century the fishmongers also had their own court of law called the Leyhalmode, where all disputes relating to fish were judged by the wardens. The company received its first royal charter in 1272. A predecessor guild had been fined as 'adulterine' – that is, illegal or unlicensed – in 1154 and other charters granted by Edward II and III maintained that no fish could be sold in London except by the 'Mystery of Fishmongers'. It took the name Stock Fishmongers' Company under another royal charter granted in 1508. Then, in 1537, it merged with the Salt Fishmongers' Company to form the Worshipful Company of Fishmongers.

Under the charter of James I the company's officials – known as 'fishmeters' – examine all fish coming into London and condemn those that have gone bad. And when bad fish is put on sale, the company institutes proceedings under the Food and Drugs Act 1955 against the offenders.

In addition to the powers granted to them by charter, the company has statutory powers under the Salmon and Freshwater Fisheries Act 1923, the Fisheries (Oyster, Crab and Lobster) Act 1877 and the Sea Fish Industry Act 1938.

The company's hall has been on its present site near the north-western corner of London Bridge since 1434. It had previously been home to a number of prominent fishmongers. The great hall there was secured for the fishmongers in 1444, giving them sole use of the accompanying wharf. The hall was destroyed by the Great Fire of London in 1666 and rebuilt in 1671; and when London Bridge was rebuilt to the west of its old site it was necessary to pull down Fishmongers' Hall. The present hall was finished in 1834.

WEAVERS

The weavers also had a court. The guild was thought to have sprung up before the Norman Conquest and is the oldest on record, with an entry on the 1130 Pipe Roll – the financial records maintained by the exchequer – for a payment of £16 made by Robert Levestan on the Weavers' behalf. Twenty-five years later the Worshipful Company of Weavers was granted a charter by Henry II which said: 'Know that I have conceded to the Weavers of London to hold their guild in London with all the liberties and customs which they had in the time of King Henry my grandfather.'

These liberties and customs included the rights to elect bailiffs, supervise the work of their craft, punish defaulters and collect the ferm – affirmation or tax. They used their court to maintain their control over the weaving trade.

In the early years of the fourteenth century the Weavers' Company submitted to the authority of the Mayor and lost its pre-eminence as other textile guilds developed, many of them powerful merchant companies such as those of the mercers, drapers, merchant taylors, haberdashers and clothworkers.

In 1321 the Court of Husting – early meetings of the City's aldermen – declared it lawful for all freemen to set up looms and sell cloth so long as the King received his yearly ferm. Edward III, who recognised the importance of the cloth trade to the nation, banned the export of wool and the import of foreign cloth. He also encouraged

Flemish weavers to bring their skills to England and prevented the weavers from forcing the foreign workers to join their guild. Instead, Flemish workers were allowed to set up their own guild. Disputes rumbled on for over a hundred years. Eventually in 1497 a pact was made absorbing the 'aliens' into the Weavers' Company.

The company's bailiffs controlled the standards and hours of work, and the arrangements for inspection and search. Wardens were concerned with the fraternal work of the guild, with charitable works and attendance at feasts and quarterly meetings, while the Court of Assistants, developed from a council of former office holders, chose the company's clerk and the beadle, and formulated general rules for the government of the craft. They also selected the liverymen from among the general body of freemen.

In 1666, Weavers' Hall burnt down, but the great chests containing the company's ancient charters were saved, along with most of the records, plate and pictures, as well as two bags of gold, which had been kept to repay debts. Funds were raised to rebuild it and on Election Day, 25 July 1669, its new hall was opened on Basinghall Street.

BASKETMAKERS

It may well be illegal to sell baskets in the City of London. Until the reign of Edward III, only freemen were allowed to do this. Their right was asserted by a number of Acts of Parliament, but Edward III allowed a number of foreign basketmakers to settle in the City.

Edward IV tried to restrict the trade again, limiting the number of apprentices and, by an Order of Council dated 1463, basketmakers were confined to Blanche Appleton, a district set aside for aliens in the parish of St Katherine Coleman in Aldgate Ward, near the present Mark Lane.

However, by the end of the fifteenth century basketmakers had moved out into the parishes of St Andrews and St Margaret Pattens. Old vestry books there list gifts or payments they made to the church. By this time, Blanche Appleton was overflowing with foreigners who were importing baskets illegally from Holland, slashing prices. In the 1517 'Evil May Day' riot, London apprentices took out their grievances on the foreigners, smashing their windows and breaking down their doors. The Lord Mayor and aldermen managed to quell the riot, but not until ten pairs of gallows were erected around the City, one in Blanche Appleton.

Then in 1538, a fire broke out in the basketmakers' premises in the parish of St Margaret Pattens. More than a dozen houses were burnt down and nine people died and, as a result, basketmakers were ordered to leave the City. They fought the order and it was suspended until 1541 when Henry VIII confirmed their expulsion.

There is no record of the expulsion order being repealed, but City records show that basketmakers had returned by 1565. Following the restoration of the monarchy in 1660, the basketmakers tried to regularise their situation by applying for a charter from the Crown to incorporate as a City livery company. Previously they had obtained their freedom by joining the Butchers' and Turners' Companies, two trades that used a lot of baskets. However, their applications to form their own company were turned down in 1682, 1685 and 1698. It was only in 1937 that the basketmakers were finally granted a royal charter by George VI. But no one knows whether they are really allowed to reside or sell their wares within the City.

SILK-THROWERS

The 1662 Silk Throwing Act establishing the City of London's Company of Silk-Throwers said that people who 'unjustly, deceitfully and falsely purloined, embezzled, pawned, sold or detained' silk and made no recompense for the loss would be subject to punishment by whipping or being put in the stocks.

Silliness in the City

Having maintained its ancient rights and
freedoms under Magna Carta, the City
felt free to enact its own laws.
A lot of these seem to have to do with
what people could wear. And, of course,
the City fathers were always watching
out for people having too much fun.

Beards and Breeches

In the reign of Henry VIII, the Court of Aldermen of the City of London took out an order against 'persons with great beards'. They were also told to 'have a vigilant eye to all the inhabitants of their wards etc using to wear outrageous breeches, etc in their apparel and to commit transgressors therein'.

Sad Days in the City

With the growth of Puritanism in the early seventeenth century, the Court of Aldermen sought to crack down on their apprentices who were having too much fun, for 'apprentices do in these days live more riotously and at their pleasures in spending their time in dancing schools, dicing-houses, tennis courts, bowling alleys, brothel-houses and other exercises unfit for their degree and calling to the high displeasure of Almighty God, wasting of their master's substance and the utter overthrow of themselves'.

Be it enacted by the authority aforesaid that every apprentice which shall be in any dancing school, or school of fencing, or learn or be dancing, or masking, or shall be dicing or any other play, or haunt any tennis court, common bowling alley, cock-fight or brothel-house, or which shall without his master's knowledge, have any chest, press, trunk, desk or any other place to lay up or keep any apparel or goods, saving only in his master's house, or by his masters' licence and appointment, or shall keep any horse, gelding, mare, dog or bitch, or fighting cock, shall upon his own confession, or proof thereof made before the chamberlain of this City (for the time being) or before any master of warden of the company whereof his master is or shall be free, be committed to Little-case for eighteen hours, or to one of the compters of the City, upon the command-ment of the Lord Mayor of this City, there to remain by the space of twenty-four hours. And for the master of such apprentice, for allowing or witting sufferance of his apprentice haunting or using any of the afore-said schools, places or exercises, shall forfeit six shillings and eight pence for every time that he shall offence therein.

Not only that, but any person living in London 'in whose hands or custody such chest, press, trunk or desk, apparel, money, ware or any other goods, horse, gelding, mare, or dog, or bitch, or fighting-cock shall be found to be kept for any such apprentice, shall forfeit and pay to the chamberlain of the City of London (for the time being) to the use of the Mayor and commonalty and citizens of the said City, the sum of forty shillings of lawful money of England, or else to abide by such punishment as shall be inflicted upon them by the Lord Mayor and court of Aldermen, agreeable to the laws of this realm'. All forfeitures, penalties and sums fined would be recovered 'by action of debt' by the King's magistrates' courts.

APPRENTICES' APPAREL

By 1611, an Act of Common Council was passed 'for reformation of apparel to be worn by apprentices, and maid-servants within the City of London, and the liberties thereof'. It specified that no apprentice could wear 'any hat lined, faced or turfed with velvet, silk or taffata ... nor any hat, other than such, as the hat and band with trimming, shall not exceed in all, the value or price of five shillings'. Neither was he to wear bands in expensive materials such as lawne or cambric, but 'holland or other linen, not exceeding the price or value of five shillings'. They were not to be edged with lace or any other work, but have plain hem with only one stitch. The material in ruff-bands were not to exceed three yards in length before they were gathered, and not to be more than two inches in depth before they were set in the stock.

Also 'no apprentice shall wear any Pickadilly' – an ornate raised collar – 'or other support, in, with, or about the collar of his doublet, nor shall wear about his collar, either point, ribbon or lace ...'. Instead collars were to be made of cloth. Doublets and breeches were not to be made out of 'any kind of silk, or stuff mingled with silk, but only of cloth, kersey, fustian, sackcloth, canvas, English leather or English stuff, which stuff shall not exceed the price or value of two shillings and six pence a yard'.

An apprentice's cloak, coat, jerkin, doublet or breeches could not be made of any broad-cloth worth more than ten shillings a yard, or kersey worth more than five shillings a yard. 'Garnishing, lining, facing' and the like were not to be made of velvet or silk, though silk buttons and buttonholes were allowed. And he was not allowed to wear gloves worth more than twelve pence a pair, and fringing or garnishing with 'gold or silver, lace, velvet, silk, or silk lace, or ribbon' was banned. Also out were any 'girdle, point, garters or shoestrings of any kind of silk or ribbon, nor any rose or such like toys at all, either on his garters or his shoes'.

After the feast day of St Michael the Archangel, apprentices were not to wear 'any silk, worsted or jersey stockings'. Woollen yarn or kersey alone were allowed. Nor could they 'wear any Spanish-leather shoes, nor any shoes made with Polonia [Polish] heels, nor any shoes made of any other leather than neat's [ox] leather or calves leather'. And their hair was to be worn without 'any tuft or lock, but cut in decent and comely manner'.

For the first offence, the apprentice would receive a simple rebuke from his master. For a second offence, the apprentice was to be brought before the chamberlain of the City and locked up for at least eighteen hours and fined three shillings and four pence, half going to the poor of the parish and half to the person who informed on him.

Fashion and Farthingales

Women's fashions was also causing the City fathers distress, so the 1611 Act also sought to avoid the 'many and great inconveniences and disorders which daily grow, by the inordinate pride of maid-servant and women servants in their excess of apparel and folly in variety of new fashions'. Consequently no maiden servant or woman servant living or working in the City of London shall 'wear up her head any lawne, cambric, tiffiny, cobweb-lawne or white silk-cipres, either in any kerchief, coif, cross-cloth or shadow, nor any linen cloth therein, saving such linen cloth only, which shall not exceed the price or value of five shillings the eln [forty-five inches]'. Lace and edging was banned. 'Bands, neckerchiefs, strippes or stomachers' all had to be plain and ruffs could not be longer than four yards before gathering, or deeper than three inches.

Also banned was 'any stomacher wrought with any gold, silver or silk or with any kind of stuff made of silk or mixed with silk'.

It was also against the law to hire a female servant wearing 'any gown, kirtle, waistcoat or petticoat, old or new, of any kind of silk stuff, or stuff mingled with silk, or any other stuff exceeding the price of two shillings and five pence a yard; nor any kersey exceeding the price of five shillings a yard; nor broadcloth exceeding the price of ten shillings a yard'. She was not to wear 'any silk lace or guard upon her grown, kirtle, waistcoat or petticoat, or any other garment, save only a cape of velvet'.

Farthingales – hoops worn to expand the hipline – were completely out and in bodices and sleeves women were not allowed wire or whalebone stiffeners, only canvas and buckram. In aprons, silk, lawne and cambric were banned, along with any material that cost more than two shillings and six pence a yard. And apron was not allowed to be more than 'one breadth' of material wide and was not allowed to have any edging, lace or fringing on it. Worsted, jersey and silk stockings were banned, along with 'any Spanish-leather shoes, shoes of any other leather, only neat's leather or calves' leather; nor any shoes whatsoever with Polonia heels; nor with the same any stitching, rose or like ribbon for shoe-strings'.

For the first offence a woman would be fined three shillings and four pence; for the second offence, five shillings and eight pence 'or the apparel worn contrary to the true meaning hereof'. Again half the fine would go to the poor of the parish and half to the informer and, if the offender did not pay up, they would be prosecuted for debt.

This Act was signed into law in 1611 and the Corporation of London does not know whether it is still in force.

THE THEATRE

Since Elizabethan times London has been famous for its theatre, but it has often fallen foul of the law. Indeed, in 1596 – during the lifetime of William Shakespeare and Ben Jonson – theatres were banned from the City of London and inns and taverns were prohibited from putting on plays, largely because the authorities feared they spread bubonic plague.

The theatres moved out to Shoreditch, just beyond the northern boundary of the City, to an area notorious for its brothels and gaming houses. The Curtain Theatre was there, where from 1597 to 1599 Shakespeare's company, the Lord Chamberlain's Men, performed, after The Theatre in the City was closed. There is still a Curtain Road in Shoreditch where the remains of the theatre were found in 2012.

Others moved across the river to Southwark, an area later famed for its bagnios (brothels). Shakespeare moved to the Globe Theatre on the South Bank when it opened there in 1599, and since 1997, the replica Shakespeare's Globe Theatre has been putting on his plays.

The 1605 Plays Act banned plays that mocked God, Christ, the Holy Ghost or the Trinity. Then under the Puritanical rule of the Commonwealth, the theatre was banned altogether, but with the Restoration of Charles II, it was soon in full bloom again.

Then, in 1713, actors, being feckless individuals, fell foul of the Vagrants Act. However, during the reigns of George II and George III, the law was amended, allowing theatres to obtain licences so that plays could be put on again. And London's theatres were specifically excluded from the Disorderly Houses Act of 1751. However, the 1737 Plays Act (full title: An Act of explain and amend so much of an act made in the twelth year of the reign of Queen Anne, intituled [*sic*]) required that new plays be submitted to the Lord Chamberlain. Even operas and pantomimes had to be submitted. The 1843 Theatres Act extended the law to dialogues between two people in costume, but not 'theatrical representations as are given in booths or shows allowed by the justices at fairs and feasts'. So the wife-beating and child abuse of a Punch and Judy show was OK. The role of the Lord Chamberlain in the theatre continued until 1968, when his office was deemed ineffective and abolished by a new Theatres Act. In 1773, local magistrates were reduced to begging the Covent Garden Theatre not to put on John Gay's *The Beggar's Opera* after an earlier production at Drury Lane had produced a spate of thieving in the area.

CITY OF LONDON SHERIFF SCAM

In 1748, the City of London came up with a wonderful money-making scam. It passed a bylaw that imposed a fine of £600 on any 'able and fit person' who, after being nominated as a City officer, refused to serve.

Under the Corporation Act of 1661 all City officials were required to swear an oath and take the sacrament under the rites of the Church of England. So the city fathers set about nominating a series of nonconformists as sheriff. As dissenters, they would refuse the sacrament. Consequently, they could not take office and would have to pay the fine.

Eventually a dissenter named Evans took the matter to the House of Lords and the practice was found to be illegal under the Toleration Act of 1689, which allowed nonconformists to worship as they chose. But in the six years the bylaw was in force, the City of London raised £15,000 – enough to build its new Mansion House, the official home of the Lord Mayor of London. Consequently the house was sometimes referred to as the Palace of Intolerance.

SWAN UPPING

As the grey waters of the Thames snake through London, there is not a swan in sight. It's true that they swim majestically around the lakes in St James's and Regent's Park, and the Serpentine in Hyde Park. But they are hardly birds you would associate with the City. Nevertheless, two City livery companies have held special rights to the swans on the Thames since the fifteenth century. As a result, there is a delightful medieval ceremony performed on the river every year.

Swans have held a unique position in English law since medieval times when they were a centrepiece dish at banquets and feasts. They have been royal birds since 1186, and are the only bird that can be 'estray' – that is, if they are found on common land or open water they belonged to the Crown as a prerogative right. The Crown can grant the privilege of keeping swans on open water provided they are marked and pinioned – that is, their wing feathers are removed so they can't fly. But if a bird strays and is not recaptured within a year and a day the ownership passes back to the Crown.

The swan's royal status was enshrined in statute with the Act of Swans 1482. This introduced a right of 'possession by prescription' and a property qualification that restricted the possession of swan mark to certain landowners and granting them a 'swan mark' to distinguish their birds. Traditionally swan marks were devices taken from the family coat of arms of the owner and cut into the upper beak with a sharp knife. They were then registered in 'swan rolls'. Once legally obtained by a grant from the Crown, these swan marks and together with the 'game of swans' marked with it, became the absolute property of the owner.

Special swanning courts known as 'swan motes' were set up to enforce the laws. Trials were presided over by a chief commissioner and decided by a jury. These courts also had the power to draw up regulations affecting swan-keeping in their area and settle disputes concerning ownership.

In 1494, Edward IV enacted 'that no one could have a game of swans' unless 'he may dispend five marks a year freehold'. Five marks in those days would be the equivalent to approximately £100. Later ordinances provided more regulations on the keeping and conservation of 'the kynges swanes and sygnettes'. One, the Case of Swans, dated 1592, gives credence to the myth that swans always sing before they die. It says: '. . . for the cock swan is the emblem of the representation of the affectionate and true husband to his wife and about all other fowls; for the cock swan holdeth himself to one female only, and for this cause nature hath conferred on him a gift beyond all others; that is to die so joyfully, that he sings sweetly when he dies'. More recently, a specific clause was included in the Wild Creatures and Forest Laws Act of 1971 to safeguard the Queen's prerogative rights over swans.

There is still a 'Master of the Swans' who is responsible to the Crown for the care of the royal swans and the general supervision of swan-keeping throughout England. The post dates from at least the fourteenth century. His job was to ensure that swans were marked and pinioned, although pinioning was stopped in 1978 after pressure from animal rights organisations. And while swan marks are no longer as elaborate as they used to be, they are still considered to be cruel and unnecessary by some conservationists and animal rights activists.

Today, the swans on the River Thames have just three owners – the Queen herself, along with the Worshipful Company of the Dyers and the Vintners. The dyers received their grant from the Crown in 1473; the vintners around 1483. Royal swans are unmarked, so the Queen owns any strays. The vintners' swans have a nick on each side of the beak, while the dyers' have a single nick on one side.

The annual marking of the swans is called 'swan upping', or sometimes 'swan hopping'. 'Upping' means taking the birds out of the water and this has been carried out on the Thames for around five hundred years. Each year the number of swans is recorded and the beaks of the new cygnets cut with the owner's swan mark. Then they are set free again.

By the eighteenth century swan upping had become an elaborate ceremony, with specially decorated boats, and the swan master and his 'swan-uppers' dressed in ceremonial costumes. It used to start at London Bridge and end at Henley, but is now restricted to the stretch of river between Walton-on-Thames and Whitchurch. On passing Windsor Castle, the rowers stand to attention in their boat with oars raised and salute 'Her Majesty The Queen, Seigneur of the Swans'.

Swan upping always takes place in the third week of July when the cygnets are about a month old and considered old enough to be handled. The Queen's swan master oversees the operation and is assisted by the swan keepers of the vintners and dyers, dressed in red, white and blue uniforms, and the boats carry the appropriate flags and pendants. They travel in traditional wooden rowing boats called barges, which are towed by motorboats for much of the journey as the upping has to be completed in five days. Each time a brood of cygnets is spotted, a cry of 'All up!' is given to signal that the boats should get into position.

The barges are manoeuvred so that the swans are trapped against the riverbank. The swans and cygnets are then carefully lifted out of the water and counted. The numbers are recorded and the cygnets are given the same ownership mark as the pen – that is, their mother. These days, they are also given a health check and ringed with individual identification numbers by the Queen's swan warden, a professor of ornithology at the University of Oxford's department of zoology. The birds are then returned to the water.

Ely Place

In the City of London, there is a small enclave guarded by beadles wearing top hats and frock coats that is technically part of Cambridgeshire. This is Ely Place, a quiet cul-de-sac near Holborn Circus, separated from the City by iron gates.

The land there was bought by John de Kirkby in 1280. Six years later, he became Bishop of Ely, which is in Cambridgeshire, and he built his palace there.

The Old Mitre tavern in Ely Court, a narrow alley-way off Ely Place, built in 1546 by Bishop Goodrich for the servants of the palace, used to have its licence issued by the Cambridge justices and it closes each night at 10 p.m. when the gates to Ely Place are shut. It still gives its address as: 'Ye Old Mitre Tavern, Ely Place, Holborn Circus, Cambridgeshire'.

Until 1939, a nightwatchman called out the hours. There was an attempt to revive the tradition after the Second World War, but there were complaints about the noise after the first night. Many of the traditional rights of the residents of Ely Place have been eroded over the years. In 1842 a local Act of Parliament established a body of commissioners 'for paving, lighting, watching, cleansing and improving Ely Place and Ely Mews'. Under the Metropolis Management Act of 1855 and later legislation, they retained their 'watching' duties, with a beadle discharging these duties. The City of London and Metropolitan Police still recognise the jurisdiction of the Cambridgeshire constabulary and do not enter Ely Place unless invited by the commissioners.

THE HIGH COST OF INFLATION

The City of London is known worldwide as a centre of banking. In 1923, a gentleman named Franklin paid a cheque for 9,000 million Deutschmarks into the Westminster Bank. It was drawn on a bank in Berlin, when Germany was undergoing runaway inflation, and he was credited £15 for it. The Westminster Bank lost out, too. By the time it presented the cheque, Germany had revalued, issuing one new Deutschmark for every one billion of the old ones. The cheque was now worth nine thousandths of a new Deutschmark, less than a tenth of penny, a transaction so small that the bank could not even be bothered with it. However, in 1929, Mr Franklin sued Westminster Bank for £459 million, claiming that the cheque was worth its face value in new Deutschmarks. After a day in court, the judge dismissed the case as 'absurd and ridiculous'. The plaintiff took the case to the Court of Appeal without success.

My Word is My Bond

Since 1801 the motto of the London Stock Exchange has been 'My word is my bond'. But this applies equally to the 'Old Lady of Threadneedle Street'.

In 1939, a wealthy Austrian who had some bearer bonds drawn on the Bank of England wanted to get them out of his country, which had just been taken over by the Nazis. He dared not risk sending them by mail or by courier in case they were intercepted. Instead he arranged for two English solicitors to meet him in a hotel room in Vienna. He showed them the bonds and told them to take careful note of the value and numbers.

Once they had done that, he asked them to watch carefully as he went over to the fireplace and burnt the bonds one by one. He then asked them to return to London and tell the Bank of England what they had seen.

There, the two solicitors made a statutory declaration that the bonds had been destroyed. Consequently, the bank issued a new set to replace them. These remained outside Austria and were available whenever the wealthy Austrian needed them.

Coal Tax

Under the Local Coal and Wine Duties Continuance Act of 1861, some 260 coal posts, or more properly coal and wine tax posts, were erected fifteen miles outside the City of London. These were the points on canals, other navigable waterways, public roads and railways when they first entered the metropolitan area. It was there that duty became payable on coal and wine coming into the City.

The Corporation of London had exercised the right of 'metage' on coal and other commodities since mediaeval times and these rights were confirmed by two charters issued by James I. The City was later permitted to set up 'a boundary stone, or some other permanent mark' where any turnpike entered the district. These taxes levied were used to rebuild St Paul's Cathedral, numerous other City churches, the Guildhall, the City's markets and Newgate Prison after the Great Fire of London.

A further Act was passed in 1694 'for the Relief of the Orphans and Other Creditors of the City of London'. This gave the City the power to impose a duty on each tun (a large cask) of wine entering the Port of London and increase the duty payable on coal. Once all debts for rebuilding the City had been repaid, surplus funds were used to finance public works, including building bridges over the Thames, paving the street and constructing new access roads into London.

Until the nineteenth century, the transport of coal and other goods into London had been by sea. But the growth of the canal and railway systems meant that collecting points for taxes had to be set up beyond the boundary of the City. So posts were erected on streams, cart tracks and footpaths. The revenue raised was used for metropolitan improvement schemes including the building of the Thames Embankment, the erection of the Holborn Viaduct and the purchase of some private Thames bridges to free them from tolls.

The tax was abolished by an Act of Parliament in 1889, but many posts remained and are now protected as Grade II-listed structures. They come in different shapes and sizes. Most are cast-iron bollards about 1.2 metres high, erected after the 1861 Act. These are normally to be found by the side of roads, but are also found in open countryside by tracks and on boundary lines. There are also granite obelisks around 1.2 metres high, erected on the banks of canals and rivers. Cast-iron boxes or plates, of about 230 millimetres square, appear built into parapets of bridges. Cast-iron or stone obelisks, just under 4.5 metres high, were built by the side of railways prior to the 1861 Act, while after the Act the small 1.5-metre cast-iron obelisks were erected beside the tracks.

Of the original 250–60 posts, 219 have survived in some form, though some have been moved to new positions. A full list can be obtained from the Corporation of London Records Office. Almost all the posts on the list can be visited, except numbers 73, 81, 219 and 165, which are inaccessible except by rail.

Justice Delayed

When James IV of Scotland became James I of England and made his way to London, he had his eye on the land occupied by Smithfield Market. It had once been a favourite place for jousting and public executions. Witches and heretics were burnt at the stake there. As far as James I was concerned, the market traders there were occupying land rent-free on long-expired leases.

In 1613, he sued in the Court of Chancery. The City of London defended vigorously, producing charters endorsed by Edward III (1327), and renewed by Henry VI (1444) and Henry VII (1505), all of which conceded the land to 'the Mayor, the Commonalty and the citizens of the City of London'.

A year later, James agreed to stay the action of the Crown v the City of London and proceedings were suspended. In 1638, his son Charles I issued another charter, but it was in Latin and without punctuation and paragraph breaks, and no one could figure out what it could mean.

The Court of Chancery dusted off the documents again in 1855 and 1860, but came to no conclusion. Meanwhile the market developed into London's great meat market.

In 1992, the market had to be redeveloped to bring it in line with European Commission food hygiene regulations. City lawyers then searched the land title records to discover who owned it, only to find that the matter had never been decided.

The case, now styled Crown Estate Commissioners v Corporation of City of London, was resumed. The Crown took the position that Charles' 1638 charter was really a long-term lease allowing land to be used by the City of London as long as it was for the purposes of a market. But at the end of the lease, the land reverted to the Crown. The charter did not, they argued, give clear title to the City of London.

The matter was then brought before Mr Justice Leonard Hoffmann, who rendered judgement on 6 May 1992.

He ruled that: 'Indeed the site was part of the Royal demesne' – the land belonged to a manor for the owner's use – 'until early in the fifteenth century, but Smithfield was indubitably included in land later given to the City under a charter granted by Henry VI in 1444 and confirmed by Henry VII in 1505.'

The Crown appealed this decision but it was upheld by Justice Mann, Evans and Nicholls of the Court of Appeal on 13 May 1994. The matter had finally been resolved after 381 years.

FIGHTING COCKS

Cockfighting was a popular sport among men and boys in London. One of the earliest accounts of the pastime being practised by schoolboys occurs in a Description of the City of London by William Fitzstephen, who wrote in the reign of Henry II and died in the year 1191. He records that it was the annual custom on Shrove Tuesday for the boys to bring their gamecocks to the schools to fight. Schoolrooms would then be turned into cockpits and the masters and pupils would spend the morning watching the birds fight.

Fighting Cocks

It appears that teachers derived much of their income from payments made by their boys for providing fighting cocks for this cruel and barbarous amusement. The masters generally claimed runaway birds and those killed in battle for the pot as perks. Cockfighting was only banned in England in 1849. Many old-school regulations and accounts contain allusions to this practice.

Tower of Bathos

Begun in 1078, the Tower of London was
built to impose Norman rule on London.
But, like all things in London, it soon
got some pretty whacky rules of its own.

THE CONSTABLE'S DUES

From the fourteenth century, every ship that came up the river to the City had to unload a portion of its cargo for the Constable of the Tower of London in recompense for enjoying the protection of the Tower's guns. When a Royal Navy ship visits the Port of London it delivers instead a barrel of rum, the traditional tipple of the navy.

As it is rare these days for the Royal Navy to steam into the Port of London, the tradition is maintained annually with the Ceremony of the Constable's Dues. Once a year the Royal Navy moors one of its ships alongside the Tower Pier, the captain delivers a barrel of rum to the constable as a symbol of these ancient rights. The captain and his escort of naval ratings are challenged at the entrance to the Tower by the yeoman gaoler, the second-in-command of the Body of Yeoman Warders, or 'Beefeaters'. They are then marched through the precincts, flanked by a contingent of yeoman warders in state dress and a corps of drum, to Tower Green, where the barrel is handed over. Afterwards the participants retire to the Queen's House – the oldest timber house in the City – to sample the contents.

Another of the constable's perks came when any horses, oxen, pigs or sheep fell off London Bridge into the moat. Owners recovering livestock from the moat had to pay a penny a foot – which usually worked out at four pence an animal – and all vegetation growing on Tower Hill belonged to the constable.

The constable was also entitled to demand six shillings and eight pence a year from the owners of all boats fishing for sprat between the Tower and the sea, one shilling a year from all ships carrying herring to London and tuppence from each pilgrim who came to London by sea to worship at the shrine of St James.

TAKING LIBERTIES

The Tower and the surrounding area known as the 'Tower of London Liberties' is independent of the City and outside the jurisdiction of both the Lord Mayor and the Bishop of London. Traditionally the liberties extended the distance of an arrow's flight from the outer walls of the Tower.

In the fourteenth century the location of the boundary markers was impressed on the minds of the local boys by giving them a severe thrashing. These days the ceremony of 'beating the bounds' is not so savage. It takes place on Ascension Day every three years when local children, armed with willow wands, beat the iron boundary markers. At each marker, the chief yeoman warder raises his mace with its ornate finial the shape of the Tower and shouts: 'Mark well!'

They sometimes confront a party from the parish of All Hallows by the Tower, who also beat their bounds that day. On one occasion, the confrontation did not turn out too well. In 1698, it is recorded that 'a most riotous assembly did muster by the walls of His Majesties Royal

Palace and Fortress of London, and protested in most vile manners at the disputed boundary betwixt the Tower and All Hallows parish church within the City of London'.

The cause of the dispute seems to have been letters patent granted by James II in 1686, expanding the Tower of London Liberties, seizing more land for the Crown. One of the boundary markers is a brass strip set into the floor of Trinity House, the other side of Trinity Square. The liberties were abolished on 25 June 1894, but the ceremony of beating the bounds continues.

RAVENS

Under a decree of Charles II six ravens must be kept in the Tower at all times. This was against the wishes of the astronomer royal, John Flamsteed, who complained that the ravens impeded the business of his observatory in the White Tower. According to legend, if the ravens left, both the Tower and the kingdom would fall. They are fed 170 grams of raw meat a day, plus bird biscuit soaked in blood, and their wings are clipped to prevent them from flying away. Nevertheless, some ravens have escaped. Others have been dismissed for bad behaviour. But the raven master keeps a seventh, spare raven on hand and there are chicks in hatcheries on site to replace any absentee. In 1675, Flamsteed moved to Greenwich, where he established the Royal Observatory.

CEREMONY OF THE KEYS

One of the best-known rites of the Tower of London has been enacted for over seven hundred years. At 9.52 p.m. precisely, the chief yeoman warder, dressed in his red Tudor watch-cloak and carrying a lantern, meets an escort of the Tower of London Guard. Together, the chief yeoman warder and the yeoman warder watchman lock the outer gate of the Tower, then the oak gates of the Middle and Byward Towers. Returning down Water Lane, they are halted by the sentry and challenged to identify themselves:

'Halt! Who comes there?' says the sentry.

'The keys,' answers the chief warder.

'Whose keys?' asks the sentry.

'Queen Elizabeth's keys,' says the chief warder, identifying the keys as those belonging to the current monarch.

'Pass Queen Elizabeth's keys. All is well,' admits the sentry.

Following this, the party makes its way through the Bloody Tower archway into the fortress. They halt at the bottom of the broadwalk steps. On the top of the stairs, the Tower guard presents arms and the chief warder raises his Tudor bonnet, announcing: 'God preserve Queen Elizabeth.' To which the sentry says: 'Amen!', exactly as the clock chimes 10 p.m. The duty drummer then sounds 'The Last Post' on his bugle, as the chief warder takes the keys to the Queen's House for safekeeping.

One night during the Second World War, the ceremony was interrupted when a bomb fell, knocking the chief yeoman warder and escort off their feet. With due aplomb, they dusted themselves off and carried on. That night, the officer of the guard wrote to George VI, apologising that the ceremony was late.

BEHEADING

Although there was once a fearsome array of 'heading axes' in the Tower, the one now kept in the Bowyer Tower is thought to be the one that removed the head of Lord Lovat who, in 1747, was the last man to be beheaded in England.

The block, usually made of oak, was originally just a piece of tree trunk. Usually it was about two feet high, so that the victim could rest their neck on it in a dignified kneeling position. Sometimes a shorter block was used deliberately to humiliate the victim. The block Charles I was executed on in Whitehall on 30 January 1649 was just ten inches tall, forcing him to lie down for his execution.

The block was rectangular with the top scalloped out on both sides. One side had a wider hollow to accommodate the prisoner's shoulders; the other side was smaller for the head. The narrow isthmus between supported the front of the neck, steadying it for the blow on the back. The blocks were usually custom made for each execution or series of executions and, again, the one in the Bowyer Tower is thought to have been made specifically for Lord Lovat.

When the head was removed with a single blow, beheading was probably the most humane form of capital punishment. Death was caused by the severing of the brain and spinal cord, and the victim also suffered severe shock and a fatal loss of blood pressure within less than sixty seconds. The question is, was it painful? It has often been reported that the eyes and mouths of people executed in this way still showed signs of movement after the head had been cut off and it has been estimated that there was enough oxygen stored in the human brain for it to continue to function for about seven seconds after the head had been severed. During that period the victim was likely to feel acute pain. However, they could lose consciousness within two to three seconds once the supply of blood to the brain had been cut off.

Between 1388 and 1747, ninety-one people were publicly beheaded outside the walls of the Tower of London on a scaffold on Tower Hill. A permanent scaffold stood there in the fifteenth and sixteenth centuries. There were just seven beheadings inside the Tower – they were all of prominent people and, consequently, well attended. Victims included Lord Hastings, who was executed during the Wars of the Roses; two wives of Henry VIII, Anne Boleyn and Catherine Howard, along with her lady-in-waiting, Lady Rochford; supporter of Catherine of Aragon Margaret Pole, Countess of Salisbury; sixteen-year-old Lady Jane Grey, who was

Queen of England for nine days in 1553, and her husband, Lord Guilford Dudley; and Robert Devereux, the second Earl of Essex and 'favourite of the Queen Elizabeth', who tried to get the people of London to revolt against her in 1601.

Curious Ceremonies

Every year, a number of bizarre
ceremonies take place in London
and are overseen by the Queen's
Remembrancer. This is now the
oldest judicial post to remain in
continuous existence since the Middle
Ages – although the post of the
Lord Chancellor is older than that of
the Remembrancer by around sixty
years, the judicial functions of the
Lord Chancellor were removed by
the Constitution Reform Act 2005.

THE QUEEN'S REMEMBRANCER

The office of King's Remembrancer originated in the Michaelmas Term of 1164 when Henry II sent his senior civil servant, Richard of Ilchester, to the Court of Exchequer to help the Treasurer – now the Chancellor of Exchequer – supervise the annual collection of taxes. His job was to 'put the King in remembrance of all things owing to the King'. After that the King's – or Queen's – Remembrancer sat in the Court of Exchequer until it was scrapped in 1882.

The Remembrancer was left with all the ceremonial duties of the court. These were laid out in the Queen's Remembrancer's Act of 1859, the Sheriffs' Act of 1887 and the Coinage Act of 1873. He is also the custodian of the Great Seal of Exchequer, which is still used on some state documents. As the last surviving member of the old Court of Exchequer, the Queen's Remembrancer has to wear a full-bottomed wig and the black tricorn hat of the former Cursitor Baron of the Court of Exchequer.

Two of the weird and ancient ceremonies the Queen's Remembrancer presides over are the Rendering of the Quit Rents to the Crown from 1211 and the Trial of the Pyx, begun in 1249.

QUIT RENTS CEREMONY

At the Quit Rents Ceremony, the Queen's Remembrancer receives the Sheriffs of the City of London, newly elected by the livery companies, and gives each of them their Warrant of Approbation from the Queen. Then the Corporation of London presents the Court of Exchequer in the person of the Remembrancer, two services for two pieces of land still in theory held by the City. In feudal times tenants would owe the lord of their manor rents and duties, which could be onerous. To be quit of these duties, agreements could be made for further payment or presentation of goods or other services. Hence the term 'quit rent'.

Between St Michael's Day (11 October) and St Martin's Day (11 November) every year the Corporation of the City of London pays quit rent for two tenancies held for over eight hundred years, although this is now only of ceremonial significance. One piece of land is known as 'The Moors' at Eardington, south of Bridgnorth in Shropshire. For this land the City presents to the Court two knives, one blunt and one sharp. These qualities are tested by the City's comptroller, who attempts to cut through a hazel rod one cubit (48 centimetres) in length and the thickness of the Remembrancer's forefinger. The rod must merely bend over the blunt knife, leaving a mark, but it must be cut through by the sharp knife. If this service is performed satisfactorily, the City could 'go quit of paying rent'. This is thought to be linked to the old use of tally sticks, when marks were made on the stick and half given to each party to the bargain.

The second quit rent is paid for a forge formerly in Tweezer's or Twizzer's Alley, just south of St Clement Danes Church in the Strand, London. It had been rented from Henry III in 1235 by a blacksmith named Walter le Brun. Back then, his shoeing shop had stood next to the jousting fields of the Knights Templar, near St Clement Danes.

This service is performed by the comptroller producing to the Remembrancer six large horseshoes and sixty-one nails, which he must count out in court before the Remembrancer pronounces 'good service'. These ceremonies date from 1295 and the horseshoes date from 1361, when the tenant of the forge was permitted to pay eighteen pence per year, provided he had made a set of horseshoes each year. In fact, the same shoes and nails are loaned by the Crown back to the City to pay the rent every year, so they are probably the oldest set of horseshoes in existence.

As part of the ceremony, the Remembrancer sits at a table covered with a chequered cloth. The cloth was used as a means for checking how much was owed by each sheriff who collected rents and the taxes due. Counters were placed on the right-hand side to show what was due, while other counters were placed on the left-hand side as the monies were paid in. This helped the Remembrancer remember and, finally, the two columns of counters should tally.

TRIAL OF THE PYX

The Queen's Remembrancer is also responsible for the annual Trial of the Pyx. This is the trial of weight and quality of the coins produced that year by the Royal Mint. It has been carried out since 1248 and has been confirmed by a series of Coinage Acts down the ages, the most recent being the Coinage Act of 1971.

In the course of the year, the Royal Mint puts aside one coin out of every 5,000 minted worth more than ten pence and one out of every 20,000 of coins worth ten pence or less. By the end of the year some 70,000 coins have been collected and placed in pyxes. These are cylindrical wooden boxes with a lid. Each February these are brought to the Goldsmiths' Hall in Foster Lane, off Gresham Street, and presented to the Queen's Remembrancer, who sits with a jury made up of the prime warden of the Worshipful Company of Goldsmiths with the three supporting wardens, the head of the Assay Office, and a selection of the company's liverymen, all in full regalia. They check the number and denomination of the coins to see that the right number has been produced. The weights and diameters of the coins are checked to see if they fall within the correct 'remedy' or tolerance required by law.

The National Weights and Measures Laboratory of the Department of Trade produce the weights for use in the trial. It also makes standard 'trial plates' of gold, silver, copper and nickel. These are cut in two in a jagged fashion. Half is supplied to the Royal Mint as a template for them to work to; the other half is used in the trial. The two halves of the trial plate can be fitted back together to prove that they are both working to the same standard and neither the Crown nor the people are being defrauded.

The coins are then assayed against pieces of metal cut from these trial plates to make sure then the fineness or composition and purity of the metal used is correct. Although gold and silver coins no longer circulate as currency in Britain, they are still produced for commemorative or ceremonial purposes such as the distribution of the Maundy Money. Each year on Maundy Thursday – the Thursday before Easter – in a ceremony that goes back to Edward I, the reigning monarch hands out a set of silver coins equal to their age to a number of people.

The actual measuring and testing of coins is done at the London Assay Office over a period of eight to ten weeks. The Trial of the Pyx reconvenes when the testing is done and the verdict of the jury is delivered each May to the Master of the Mint, or his deputy, and the Queen's Remembrancer, hopefully, confirming that the coinage of the realm is sound for another year. According to law:

> The verdict of the jury shall be in writing and signed by each of the jurymen and shall be handed to the Queen's Remembrancer, who shall authenticate it with his signature, deposit it with the records of his office and deliver a copy of it to the Treasury. The Queen's Remembrancer shall direct that the verdict, or those parts of the verdict which he considers appropriate, shall be read aloud in his presence. The

Treasury shall deliver one copy of the verdict to the proper officers of the Department of Trade and Industry and another copy to the Deputy Master of the Mint and shall cause the verdict to be published in the *London Gazette*.

Originally the trial was needed to check that the Master of the Mint was not cheating. These days, of course, the weight, size and composition of British coins are checked by machine at the Royal Mint.

Although the verdict of the Trial of the Pyx may seem like a foregone conclusion, in 1710 the jury reported that the coins had fallen below standard. But the then Master of the Mint, Sir Isaac Newton, was able to show that the trial plate of 1707 had been made too fine. He managed to get it withdrawn and the Mint returned to the trial plate of 1688.

After 1837, the old trial plates were stored, along with old coinage dies, in the Pyx Chapel in the cloisters of Westminster Abbey, which dates from the reign of William the Conqueror. The earliest surviving trial plate is a silver ingot dating from 1278 or 1279. The Chapel houses a virtually unbroken series of gold and silver trial plates from 1477 onwards, including the disputed 1707 plate. However, there is only a tiny fragment left of the 1688 trial plate, after its reuse.

NOMINATION OF THE HIGH SHERIFF

The Remembrancer also supervises the nomination of High Sheriffs, including the High Sheriff of Greater London. He reads the roll of those nominated to the Queen. The roll is a continuous sheet of paper about twenty-three feet long. Under the Sheriffs Act 1887, this must be prepared by 12 November each year. It is submitted to the Queen at a meeting of the Privy Council the following February or March to prick the name of her choice by means of a silver bodkin. By convention she pricks the first name on the roll.

PRESENTATION OF THE LORD MAYOR OF LONDON

Each November on Lord Mayor's Day, it is the Remembrancer's job to present the new Lord Mayor of London to the Lord Chief Justice and the Master of the Rolls and the other judges at the Royal Courts of Justice in the Strand. He administers to the Lord Mayor his oath or 'declaration of office' to faithfully perform the duties of Lord Mayor. This is inscribed on an illuminated vellum document, which he and the Remembrancer sign. After that the Lord Mayor returns to the Mansion House as part of the annual Lord Mayor's Show.

West End Wackiness

Weird stuff does not just go on in
the City, where it is understandable,
even excusable, because of its
antiquity. The West End is much
younger, but there is still a world
of wacky goings-on there, too.

BURLINGTON ARCADE

In the West End, there is another small enclave, with its own jurisdiction, a mile-and-a-half to the west, called Burlington Arcade. It is a covered mall of tiny shops, many with their original signs, that runs for 196 yards between Piccadilly and Old Burlington Street, where the laws of the Regency still apply.

The arcade was built in 1818 by Lord George Cavendish, later to become the Earl of Burlington, and designed by architect Samuel Ware 'for the sale of jewellery and fancy articles of fashionable demand, for the gratification of the public'. From the moment the gates were first thrown open in 1819, it was an instant success with the fashionable ladies and dandies of the day.

Nearly two centuries later, Burlington Arcade retains Regency decorum by banning singing, humming, whistling, hurrying and 'behaving boisterously'. The laws are enforced by a corps of Burlington Arcade Beadles, originally recruited by Lord Cavendish from his regiment, the Tenth Hussars. Things have moved on, however. Today the beadles wear Edwardian frock coats, gold buttons and gold-braided top hats.

It seems that the ban on singing and whistling was enforced because pimps used to burst into song or whistle to warn prostitutes who were soliciting in the arcade that the police or beadles were about. The prostitutes working on the upper level would also whistle to the pickpockets below to warn them of approaching police. This rule is still rigidly enforced, though it is said that Sir Paul McCartney is the one person who is currently exempt.

The laws have had to change with the times, too: originally it was forbidden to carry a parcel in the arcade, but modern shoppers want to take their purchases home with them.

TOP HAT

Who would have through that Fred Astaire would have been an incorrigible law-breaker? But when he was putting on his top hat, tying up his white tie and brushing off his tails, he was breaking the law – in London at least.

The precedent was set in 1797 when the inventor of the top hat, London haberdasher John Hetherington, decided to give his new hat its public debut, left his shop in the Strand and went for a drive through the City. The sight of his hat caused a sensation. People booed. Several women fainted. A crowd gathered and a small boy got his arm broken in the crush.

Hetherington was arrested, arraigned before the Lord Mayor of London and charged with conduct likely to cause a breach of the King's peace. He was charged with 'appearing on the public highway wearing upon his head a tall structure having a shining lustre and calculated to frighten timid people'. Officers of the Crown stated that 'several women fainted at the unusual sight, while children screamed, dogs yelped and a younger son of Cordwainer Thomas was thrown down by the crowd which collected and had his right arm broken'. Found guilty, Hetherington was fined £50, an enormous sum in those days.

SPEAKERS' CORNER

The American Revolution was extremely popular in England, and in London there were several attempts to overthrow the monarchy. These were renewed in the wake of the French Revolution by so-called Jacobin alehouse clubs. In an attempt to quell insurrection, Parliament passed a number of Seditious Meetings Acts, which limited the size of any meeting to fifty people and insisted that organisers give six days' notice of the event. But there was an unexpected loophole. While it was all very well to pass an Act limiting meetings in public places, in London the royal parks belong to the Crown, so are, in fact, private property. In 1856, law officers informed the government that they could only eject people from the royal parks using the laws of trespass, which meant they could not use unreasonable force to make people leave if they refused to do so, as manhandling them would constitute assault. Nor could the police order a meeting to disperse. People could only be removed from private property if notice of their eviction was served on each of them individually.

In recognition of this, the Parks Regulation Act was passed in 1872. It set aside a portion of each park for public meetings. The result was Speakers' Corner at the north-east of Hyde Park opposite Marble Arch. Meanwhile the Seditious Meetings Act had fallen into disuse and it was repealed by the Public Order Act of 1986. This also repealed the Tumultuous Petitioning Act of 1661 – 'An Act against Tumults and Disorders upon pretence of preparing or presenting publick petitions or other Addresses to His Majesty or the Parliament'. It said that no petition or address could be presented to the King or either House of Parliament by more than ten persons. Nor could you get more than twenty persons to petition for the alteration of any matters established by law of the Church or State, unless you got the consent of three justices of the county, or the major part of the grand jury. Not much of a petition then if it is signed by just twenty people.

BATH CHAIRS

In the late-Victorian era, a law was passed that banned bath chairs – once the favoured mode of transport of the elderly and gout-ridden – being pushed three abreast in area of St James's and Green Park. It seems that the Victorian gentry were presenting the sort of hazard caused by skateboarders today.

IMPERSONATING A BUILDING

The owners of the Royal Albert Hall in Kensington sought an injunction to restrain a Mr Albert Edward Hall from calling his band the Albert Hall Orchestra, on the grounds that the public were fooled into thinking that his orchestra was in some way connected with their building. As at the time the Royal Albert Hall had no orchestra of its own, there was no evidence of injury, so the injunction was denied.

BILL STICKERS

The Public Order Act 1986 makes it an offence punishable with a fine of up to £400 to display 'any writing, sign or other visible representation which is threatening, abusive or insulting thereby causing that or another person harassment, alarm or distress'.

Three days before the election in 1987, a policeman on patrol in Kensington High Street caught a fly poster in the act. The poster he was intending to stick on the wall depicted Prime Minister Margaret Thatcher in fishnet stockings and suspenders, wielding a whip. Under her were the words, 'On your knees to Madam M. You must make up your mind – do you want to work with madam or not?'

The policeman thought that this was abusive and insulting within the meaning of the Act and brought charges. But cross-examined in court, the PC admitted that he had found the poster funny, though not hilarious. As the prosecution failed to produce anyone who had been harassed, alarmed or distressed by the poster, the magistrates ruled that there was no case to answer.

Legal Lampoonery

The British judiciary are notorious for
their strange regalia. Until quite recently,
a man could be arrested for walking
down the street wearing a wig, a robe and
silk stockings – unless he was a judge.
But then some might argue that many
judges throughout history have chosen
to make up the rules as they go along.

JUDGE'S HEADGEAR

English judges have not always worn wigs. In the reigns of James I and Charles I, they appeared with their own hair. It was John Bradshaw – president of the court in Westminster Hall that condemned Charles I to death – who began the fashion for wearing novel headgear. For the occasion, he wore a thick-crowned beaver hat with a steel plate inside it to 'ward off blows in the event of public tumult'. After that the Lord Chancellor and Speaker of the House of Commons took to wearing round-crowned beaver hats.

Then, with the Restoration, Charles II and his courtiers brought the fashion from the Continent for luxuriant wigs and three-cornered cocked hats. Barristers began to do the same, but very gradually, 'for judges at first thought them so coxcombical that they would not suffer young aspirants to plead before them so attired,' said Lord Campbell, the Lord Chancellor. 'Who would have supposed that this grotesque ornament, fit only for an African chief, would be considered indispensably necessary for the administration of justice in the middle of the nineteenth century?'

Lady Eldon, the wife of the Lord Chancellor under George III, disliked wigs. To please her, Lord Eldon asked the King whether, when not sitting in court, he might appear with his own hair, pointing out that judges had done so before the Interregnum.

'True,' said the King. 'I admit the correctness of your statement, and am willing, if you like it, that you should do as they did; for, though they certainly had no wigs, yet they wore long beards.'

There were, of course, changing fashions in wigs. When the American academic lawyer and senator from Massachusetts visited London in 1838 and mixed with the leading judges and counsels, he noted: 'Lord Denman, C.J. [Chief Justice], then considered the wigs the silliest thing in England. I took the liberty of telling this to Justice Allan Park, who at once exclaimed that it was all a piece of Denman's coxcombry: that he just wished to show off his own person. A few years ago, when an invention came out by means of which wigs were made with the appearance of being powdered and yet without powder, and without the consequent dirt, Park resisted the change as an innovation on the constitution; he actually refused to recognise his own son at the bar when appeared in one of the new fangled wigs.'

THE OFFICIAL COSTUME OF THE BAR

During the reign of Mary, the lawyers devoted much of their attention to the regulation of their own dress and personal appearance. To check what they saw as 'the grievance of long beards', an order was issued by the Inner Temple, 'that no fellow of that house should wear his beard above three weeks' growth, on pain of forfeiting 20s'. The Middle Temple enacted, 'that none of that society should wear great breeches in their hose, made after the Dutch, Spanish or Almain [German] fashion, or lawn upon their caps, or cut doublets, under a penalty of 3s. 4d., and expulsion for the second offence'. In 1556 it was ordained by all the Inns of Court, 'that none except knights and benchers should wear in their doublets or hose any light colours, save scarlet and crimson, nor wear any upper velvet cap, or any scarf or wings in their gowns, white jerkins, buskins, or velvet shoes, double cuffs in their shirts, feathers or ribbons in their caps, and that none should wear their study gowns in the city any farther than Fleet Bridge or Holborn Bridge; nor while in commons wear Spanish cloaks, sword and buckler, or rapier, or gowns and hats, or gowns girded with a dagger on the back'.

NAKED JUSTICE

Though judges and barristers love their wigs and gowns, according to High Court judge and historian Sir Robert Megarry, 'robes are not essential, and the court may dispense with them when there is good reason. Jurisdiction is neither conferred nor excluded by mere matters of attire or locality, and I need not discuss the numberless occasions on which judges have exercised a variety of judicial functions in unusual places without the aid of robes for them or my counsel from Lord Lyndhurst L.C. in a box at the opera to Sir Lancelot Shadwell V.C. while bathing in the Thames and Sir Samuel Evans P. in a dressing-gown in his bedroom.'

THE LITTLE INNS OF COURT

These days, London boasts only four Inns of Court – Lincoln's Inn, Gray's Inn, Middle Temple and Inner Temple. This is where barristers for England and Wales reside. Law students qualify there if they attend – these days – just twelve dinners in the chosen inn. It used to be twenty-four. Although US Chief Justice Warren Burger tried to set up Inns of Court in America, no American city has more than one, so the ancient Inns of Court remain thoroughly Londonesque institutions. However, the Inns of Court are not in London itself. A decree of Henry III (1216–72) banned institutions of legal education from the City, so they set up outside in the small village of Holborn, now a busy part of the conurbation between the City and the West End.

The inns and lodging houses there were home to the barristers. Although only four inns remain, there were once other smaller inns that have long since disappeared. Usually they bore the name of the original landlord. In the 1850s, a Royal Commission was set up to look into them. However, this did so little to clear away the dust and cobwebs that these smaller inns remained, in the words of Lord Dundreary, 'things that no fellow can understand'.

LYON'S INN

Lyon's Inn was founded in or before the reign of Henry V (1413–22). Some distinguished lawyers practised there during the reign of Elizabeth I (1558–1603), but it was demolished in 1863 to make way for a theatre 'without any person evincing the smallest interest in its late'. The theatre itself was demolished in 1902 to make way for the construction of Bush House and the Aldwych.

All that the Royal Commission could discover about Lyon's Inn came from the evidence of Timothy Tyrrell, who said he believed that it consisted of members or 'ancients' – he could not say which as he believed the terms were synonymous. He was one of them and there was only one other. Within his recollection there had never been more than five, and they had nothing to do beyond receiving the rents of the chambers.

There were no students, and the only payment made on account of legal instruction was a sum of £7 13s. 4d. paid to the society of the Inner Temple for a reader. But there had been no reader since 1832; Tyrrell said he had heard his father say that the reader 'burlesqued the things so greatly' that the ancients were disgusted, and would not have another. There was a hall, but it was used only by a debating society, and there was a kitchen attached to it, but he had never heard of the inn having a library.

NEW INN

New Inn appears to have been somewhat more alive than Lyon's, although it does not seem to have done any more to advance the cause of legal education. It was one of the Inns of Chancery that stopped training barristers at the beginning of the Civil War in 1642. The property held was taken over by the Middle Temple on a three-hundred-year lease, beginning in 1744, at a rent of four pounds a year. Among the stipulations of the lease, the lessors retained the right to hold lectures in the hall, but none had been held since 1846. It was thought this was because the Middle Temple had ceased sending a reader. There had never been more than five or six lectures a year and by the time of the Royal Commission no legal education was provided.

Representing the inn before the Royal Commission, Samuel Brown Jackson said he knew nothing about any ancient deeds or documents that would throw any light on the original constitution and functions of the institution. If there were any, he said he supposed they were in the custody of the Treasurer. The only source of income was the rents of chambers, which then amounted to between eighteen and nineteen hundred pounds a year. The ancients had no duties beyond the administration of the funds.

Clement's Inn

Representing Clement's Inn, Thomas Gregory, the steward of the society there, said he was unable to afford full information, but he had seen papers dating back to 1677, when there was a conveyance by Lord Clare to one Killett. This was followed by a Chancery suit between the latter and the principal and ancients of the society. As a result, it was decreed that the property conveyed became vested in the inn.

Some of the papers relating to the inn had been lost by fire, and 'some of them we can't read', said Gregory. The inn, he believed, was formerly a monastery, and took its name from St Clement. It had once been in connection with the Inner Temple, but he could find no papers showing what were the relations between the two societies, 'except that a reader comes once a term, but that was dropped for twenty years – I think till about two or three years ago, and then we applied to them ourselves, and they knew nothing at all about it; the under-treasurer said he did not know anything about the reader, and had forgotten all about it'.

It was the custom for the Inner Temple to submit three names to the ancients.

'We chose one,' said the witness. 'But then they said that the gentleman was out of town, or away, and that there was no time to appoint another.'

In the cause of legal education, this was no great loss as it appeared that all a reader had ever done was to explain some recent Act of Parliament to the ancients and commoners, there being no students. The inn had no library and no chapel – as a substitute it had three pews in the neighbouring church of St Clement. It also had a vault where, the witness said, 'the principals or ancients may be buried if they wish it'. It was the last of the Inns of Chancery to be shut down in 1903 for the Aldwych development.

STAPLES INN

Things proved even more confusing when the Royal Commission looked into the affairs of Staples Inn, even though Edward Rowland Pickering, the author of a book on the subject, testified to the Royal Commission and one of the commissioners had a copy of the book in front of him while the witness was under examination.

'You state here,' said the commissioner, 'that in the reign of Henry V, or before, the society probably became an Inn of Chancery, and that it is a society still possessing the manuscripts of its orders and constitutions.'

'I am afraid,' replied Pickering, 'that the manuscript is lost. The principal has a set of chambers which were burnt down, and his servant and two children were burnt to death, seventy years ago; and I rather think that these manuscripts might be lost.'

It was not clear where Pickering had got the information for his book from. Asked whether he knew of any trace of a connection between the society and another Inn of Court, he replied: 'Certainly, I should say not. It is sixty years since I was there, boy and all.'

During the sixty years he had been connected or acquainted with the society, he had never heard of the existence of a reader, or of any association of the inn with legal education or legal pursuits. The only connection claimed for the inn by the principal, Andrew Snape Thorndike, was that, when a serjeant or senior barrister was called from Gray's Inn, Staples Inn were invited to breakfast.

Tenure of chambers in the inn ran indefinitely. 'A person holds them for his own life,' said Thorndike, 'and though he may be seventy years of age, if he can come into the hall, he may surrender them to a very young man, and if that young man should live he may surrender them again at the same age.'

If the chambers were not surrendered, they reverted to the society on the tenant's death.

Barnard's Inn

Barnard's Inn dates back at least to the mid-thirteenth century. The property had been held on lease from the dean and chapter of Lincoln for more than three hundred years. The society consists of a principal, nine ancients and five companions, who were chosen by the ancients. The evidence of Charles Edward Hunt, treasurer and secretary of the inn, failed to make it clear how the ancients chose them. However, it was clear that applications for admission by solicitors were not allowed. This had happened once, in 1827.

'Of course, we refused him,' said Hunt, 'and he applied to the court, and after some difficulty he got a rule nisi for a mandamus. It came on to be tried before Lord Tenterden, and Lord Tenterden said it could not be granted; that we were a voluntary association, and the court had no jurisdiction.'

The applicant seems to have based his claim on the grounds that Barnard's was an Inn of Chancery, and that, as a solicitor, he had a right to be admitted. The matter was scarcely worth contention, as the privileges of the companions were confined to dining in hall and the chance of being made an ancient, that favoured grade being entitled to 'their dinners and some little fees'.

The books of the society showed no trace of there ever having been any students of law connected with the inn.

'The oldest thing I find,' said the witness, 'is that a reader came occasionally from Gray's Inn to read; but what he read about, or who paid him, there is no minute whatever.'

Hunt did not know when a reader last came from Gray's Inn. He thought it was about two hundred years earlier. Barnard's Inn did not have a library. There had been a few books at one time, the witness told the Royal Commission, but they were sold as useless.

Barnard's Inn is now home to Gresham College, Holborn.

CLIFFORD'S, SYMOND'S AND FURNIVAL'S INNS

No evidence was taken by the Royal Commission concerning Clifford's, Symond's and Furnival's Inns. They appeared to be merely residential chambers and were not being used exclusively by members of the legal profession. In the 1840s a retired army officer was occupying chambers in Clifford's Inn, while a curate resided in Symond's Inn with his wife and a young family.

Michael Doyle, who represented Lincoln's Inn before the Royal Commission, said that the society in Furnival's Inn received £576 a year under a lease of the former property granted to the late Henry Peto for ninety-nine years, £500 being for rent and the remainder in lieu of land tax. But he did not know when the property was acquired by Lincoln's Inn. Sir Thomas More had been reader there from 1504 to 1507. Charles Dickens lived there from 1834 to 1837, when he began writing *The Pickwick Papers*. J. M. Barrie also lived there from 1888 to 1889. The building was demolished in 1897 to make way for Gamages department store. That closed in 1972 and the site is now Holborn Bars.

The inquiry by the Royal Commission resulted in the recommendation of some radical changes in the constitution of the little Inns of Court, but these made very little difference. The inns had long outlived the purposes. Although their principals and officials seem to attach considerable importance to their continued existence, they were shut down or amalgamated into the larger inns.

SEEDS OF REVOLUTION

It seems strange that, with the Inns of Court being such a central part of the establishment, it should ally itself with rebels to the Crown. Through his education, Thomas Jefferson had ties with the Middle Temple and a copy of the Declaration of Independence hangs in the

Middle Temple. It is signed by five Middle Templars –
one of them, John Rutledge, went on to draft the US
Constitution.

THE POLITE JUDGE

Sitting in the Old Bailey in the 1890s, Mr Justice
Graham was known as 'the polite judge'. One day,
he was sentencing sixteen prisoners to death,
largely for petty theft. Fellow judge Sir Henry
Hawkins recorded:

> His lordship, instead of reading the whole of the
> sixteen names, omitted one, and read out only fifteen.
> He then politely, and with exquisite precision and
> solemnity, exhorted them severally to prepare for
> the awful doom that awaited them the following
> Monday, and pronounced on each the sentence of
> death.
>
> They left the dock.
>
> After they were gone the gaoler explained to his
> lordship that there had been sixteen prisoners capi-
> tally convicted, but that his lordship had omitted the
> name of one of them, and he would like to know what
> was to be done with him.
>
> 'What is the prisoner's name?' asked Graham.
>
> 'John Robins, My Lord.'
>
> 'Oh, bring John Robins back by all means. Let
> John Robins step forward. I am obliged to you.'

The culprit was once more placed at the bar, and Graham, addressing him in his singularly courteous manner, said apologetically: 'John Robins, I find I have accidentally omitted your name in my list of prisoners doomed to execution. It was quite accidental, I assure you, and I ask your pardon for my mistake. I am very sorry, and can only add that you will be hanged with the rest.'

QUICK-FIRE JUSTICE

In the nineteenth century, the Old Bailey sat until five o'clock, then the senior judges went to a sumptuous dinner provided by the Lord Mayor and the aldermen, where they drank everyone's health but their own. There was another dinner for the recorder, the common serjeant and others at six o'clock. The chaplain of Newgate Prison, whose job it was to say 'Amen' when a sentence of death had been announced, attended both. Well refreshed, the official returned to the courtrooms to dispense more justice.

It was noted that 'after-dinner trials' occupied an average of less than four minutes each. However, Sir Henry Hawkins, later Lord Brampton, recorded one trial at the Old Bailey in the 1840s that took just two minutes fifty-three seconds.

Prosecuting counsel: I think you were walking up Ludgate Hill on Thursday the twenty-fifth, about half-past two in the afternoon and suddenly felt a tug at your pocket and missed your handkerchief which the constable now produces? Is that it?

Witness: Yes, sir.

Judge to the defendant: I suppose you have nothing to ask him? . . . Next witness.

The constable stands up.

Prosecuting counsel: Were you following the prosecutor on the occasion when he was robbed on Ludgate Hill? And did you see the prisoner put his hand into the prosecutor's pocket and take this handkerchief out of it?

Constable: Yes, sir.

Judge to the defendant: Nothing to say, I suppose?

Judge to jury: Gentlemen, I suppose you have no doubt? I have none.

Jury: Guilty, my lord.

Judge to defendant: Jones, we have met before. We shall not meet again for some time. Seven years' transportation. Next case.

The Wages of Sin

According to Robert Megarry, the rebuilding of the Old Hall in Lincoln's Inn was partly paid for by fining barristers six shillings and eight pence for 'fornicating with a woman in chambers'. The fine rose to twenty shillings 'if he shall have or enjoy her in the garden or Chancery Lane'.

DREGS OF THE PEOPLE

When Sir Peter Laurie, a saddler, became Lord Mayor of London, he gave a dinner in the Mansion House for the judges. Proposing a toast to their health, he said: 'What a country is this we live in. In other parts of the world there is not a chance, except for men of high birth and aristocratic connexions; but here genius and industry are sure to be rewarded. See before you the examples of myself, the Chief Magistrate of the metropolis of this great empire, and the Chief Justice of England sitting at my right hand [Lord Tenterden], both now in the very highest offices in the state, and both sprung from the very dregs of the people.'

A PROPER PROCESSION

English judges love a good procession through the streets of London. When the Earl of Shaftesbury became Lord Chancellor in 1672, he promised the capital a sight it had not seen for over half a century. At the opening of a term, the Chancellor and the judges would formerly ride on horseback to the Westminster

Hall, but in the last years of the reign of Elizabeth I carriages had been introduced.

The new innovation soon found favour with the judiciary. The Chancellor headed the procession in a grand gilt carriage, almost as large as a house. He was followed by the judges, king's serjeants, king's counsels, clerks and other court officials, riding in modern equipages. But Shaftesbury was determined to bring back the horseback procession.

Judges who went out on the circuit were used to riding, but those who inhabited the Inns of Court were not, as, by then, the habit of riding horses in the streets of London had fallen into disuse. However, Shaftesbury had been bred a country squire and had then served as the colonel of a regiment of cavalry. He prided himself on his horsemanship and wanted to take revenge on older judges who he heard had been sneering at his decisions.

On the first day of Hilary Term in January 1673, he ordered that there would be a 'judicial cavalcade', according to ancient practice, from his residence in Exeter House in the Strand to Westminster.

That morning he gave a sumptuous breakfast not only to the peers, noblemen, judges and other dignitaries, but also to all the barristers, the students at the Inns of Court and the sixty clerks and other officers of the Court of Chancery. Well fed and watered, Shaftesbury mounted his richly caparisoned charger. His insignia of office was carried before him, while his master of the horse, page, groom and six footmen walked alongside.

The procession travelled up the Strand, through the quadrangle at Whitehall and into King Street, then the only entrance to Palace Yard, and on to Westminster Hall. All did not go well. According to one account, seventy-one-year-old Lord Twisden, who presided at the trial of the regicides, 'in his great affright, and to the consternation of his grave brethren, was laid along in the dirt; but all at length arrived safe, without loss of life or limb in the service. This accident was enough to divert the like frolic for the future, and the very next term after, they fell to their coaches as before.'

A Dinner Party at the London Chancellor's

In his diary, Sir John Reresby records:

On 18th January, 1685, I dined with the Lord Chancellor Jeffreys, where the Lord Mayor of London was a guest, and some other gentlemen. His lordship having, according to custom, drank deep at dinner, called for one Montfort, a gentleman of his who had been a comedian, an excellent mimic, and to divert the company, as he was pleased to term it, he made him plead before him in a feigned cause, during which he aped all the great lawyers of the age, in their tone of voice, and in their action and gesture of body, to the very great ridicule, not only of the lawyers, but of the law itself, which to me did not seem altogether so prudent in a man of lofty station in the law. Diverting it certainly was, but prudent in the Lord Chancellor I shall never think it.

THE GREAT SEAL

The Great Seal of England – later the Great Seal of the United Kingdom – must be affixed to an official document of state to make it law. The Keeper of the Great Seal is the Lord Chancellor.

Lord Chancellor Nottingham used to take it to bed with him. So when his house in Queen Street was robbed on 7 November 1677, the thief, one Thomas Sadler, did not find it because it was tucked under his pillow. Sadler was later arrested and hanged at Tyburn.

In the Glorious Revolution of 1688, while fleeing, the deposed James II dropped the Great Seal in the Thames, believing that the new administration could not make laws without it. However, it caught in the nets of a fisherman near Lambeth and he returned it.

It was then stolen from Lord Thurlow's house in Great Ormond Street on 24 March 1784. A reward was offered, but it was never traced and the lawmakers have continued unimpeded.

Tenue de nuit.

The Metropolitan Police

The streets of London were always
a dangerous place and after the
Restoration in 1660 gangs proliferated.
One of these gangs called themselves
The Bloods – a name now adopted
by a street gang originating in the
Compton district of Los Angeles.

LAWLESSNESS

The historian Thomas Macaulay wrote of the dangers of walking the streets of London's West End during the Restoration: 'When the evening closed in, the difficulty and danger of walking about London became serious indeed. The garret windows were opened and pails were emptied, with little regard to those who were passing below. Falls, bruises and broken bones were of constant occurrence; for, till the last year of the reign of Charles II, most of the streets were left in profound darkness. Thieves and robbers plied their trade with impunity; yet they were hardly so terrible to peaceful citizens as another class of ruffians. It was a favourite amusement of dissolute young gentlemen to swagger by night about the town, breaking windows, upsetting sedans, beating quiet men, and offering rude caresses to pretty women.'

THIEFTAKERS

By the early part of the eighteenth century, policing in London was in the hands of the thieftakers. At the time constables and justices were either paid very poorly, or not at all and lived off fees paid by victims. This became an organised racket. The most successful thieftaker was Jonathan Wild, who arranged to have goods stolen so he could sell them back to their owners. Anyone who opposed him was betrayed to the authorities. It is thought that some 120 went to the gallows on Wild's say so. After some fifteen years as 'thieftaker general', Wild was convicted of a minor felony and hanged.

In 1748, the writer Henry Fielding was appointed justice of the peace for Westminster and Middlesex, with his courthouse, which was also his home, in Bow Street. While practising as a lawyer, Fielding's literary career flourished and he wrote *The Life of Mr Jonathan Wild the Great*. With no interest in taking fees, or bribes, for his work as a magistrate, he put an advertisement in *The Covent-Garden Journal* that read: 'All persons who shall for the future suffer by robbers, burglars, etc., are desired immediately to bring or send the best description they can of such robbers, etc., with the time, and place, and circumstances of the fact, to Henry Fielding, Esq., at this house in Bow Street.'

Fielding found the constables who patrolled the City so incompetent that he sacked them and hired six men of his own. These became the Bow Street Runners. Their success in capturing highwaymen encouraged the government to give him the money to increase his squad to ten. When Fielding died in 1754, his blind brother John took over. Although he was equally successful in stamping out the gangs of highway robbers who preyed on travellers on the turnpikes around the City, the government withdrew funding and soon crime returned to its former levels.

The situation became so dire that in 1829 Home Secretary Sir Robert Peel sponsored the Metropolitan Police Act that expanded the police force to cover the whole of the metropolitan area – from Camberwell in the south to Highgate in the north – and established the

London Metropolitan Police Department. With a hierarchy of rank in military fashion, this became the model for police forces in the rest of the country, the Commonwealth and the United States. Policemen in London became known as Peelers or Bobbies after their founder.

METROPOLITAN POLICE ACT OF 1829

This Act carried some strange provisions. Clause VI, for example, read: 'Penalty on publicans harbouring police men' and cut down on coppers' jollies. It says that 'if any victualler or keeper of any house, shop, room or other place for the sale of liquors, which spirituous or otherwise, shall knowingly harbour or entertain any man belonging to the said police force, or permit such man to abide or remain in the house, shop, room, or other place during any part of the time appointed for his being on duty, every such victualler or keeper as aforesaid, being convicted thereof before any two Justices of the Peace, shall for every such offence forfeit and pay such a sum, not exceeding five pounds, as they shall think meet'. In other words, the poor old publican was to be punished, not the drunken policeman.

OUTLAW KIDS

The catch-all Metropolitan Police Act of 1839 prohibiting the rolling of 'any cask, tub, hoop, or wheel ... on any footway, except for the purpose of loading or unloading any cart or carriage'. Children are not allowed to fly a kite 'or play at any game to the annoyance of the inhabitants'. Nor can they 'slide upon ice or snow', set off fireworks, build bonfires or ring doorbells 'without lawful excuse, or ... wilfully extinguish the light of any lamp'.

BEATING MATS

Under section 60, paragraph three of the Act, it is an offence to 'beat or shake any carpet, rug or mat in any street in the Metropolitan Police District'. The penalty is a fine of £2. It is, however, permitted to shake out a doormat, as long as you do so before eight o'clock in the morning. This paragraph also covers the waste from slaughterhouses. It is also against the law to hang beds out of windows.

EMPTYING THE PRIVY

The next paragraph imposes a similar fine on 'every person who shall empty or begin to empty a privy between the hours of six in the morning and twelve at night, or remove along any thoroughfare any night soil, soap lees, ammoniacal liquor or other such offensive matter, between the hours of six in the morning and eight in the evening, or who shall at any time use for any such purpose any cart or carriage not having a proper covering, or who shall carelessly slop or spill any such offensive matter'. There is, of course, a caveat for those on official business: 'This enactment shall not be construed to prevent the commissioner of any sewers within the Metropolitan Police District, or any person acting in the service or by their direction, from emptying or removing along any thoroughfare at any time the contents of any sewer which they are authorised to cleanse or empty'.

PIGSTIES

Londoners are not allowed to keep a pigsty in the front of their houses. This section is still in force, but the chapter preventing you from heating or melting 'pitch, fat, rosin, grease, tallow, oil or other combustible matter' on board a ship between Westminster Bridge and Blackwall has been repealed. So that's all right then.

PROFANE SONGS

You are not allowed to 'sing any profane, indecent or obscene song or ballad, or write or draw any indecent or obscene word, figure or representation, or use any profane, indecent or obscene language'. So just about any City trader could be locked up on Friday night after the markets close. Nor are you allowed to 'blow any horn' unless you are a guard or a postman belonging to Her Majesty's post office in the performance of their duty.

BEAR-BAITING

Under the 1839 Act no person within the Metropolitan Police District 'shall keep or use, or act in the management of any house, room, pit, or other place for the purpose of fighting or baiting lions, bears, badgers, cocks, dogs, or other animals'. The penalty was a fine of up to £5, with up to one month in gaol with or without hard labour. Like much of the 1839 Act, this section is still in force – although there is no record of anyone being so foolhardy to bait a bear within the Metropolitan district recently.

CATTLE AND HORSES

Londoners can herd cattle along the streets, provided they do not 'wantonly and unlawfully pelt, drive or hunt any such cattle'. However, it was illegal to 'feed or fodder any horse or other animal, or show any caravan containing any animal, or any other show or public entertainment, or shoe, bleed, or farry any horse or animal, or clean, dress, exercise, train, or break any horse or animal . . . in any thoroughfare or public places'.

The slaughtering or dressing of cattle in the streets is illegal, except if the animal concerned has been run over by the person who is doing the slaughtering or dressing, while it is forbidden under the Metropolitan Streets Act of 1867 to drive cattle down the roadway between 10 a.m. and 7 p.m. without prior approval from the Commissioner of Police.

GUNS AND EXPLOSIVES

It is unlawful to 'discharge any cannon or other firearm of greater calibre than a common fowling piece within three hundred yards of any dwelling house within the said district to the annoyance of any inhabitant thereof'. And it is illegal for anyone in London who 'lives within a mile of any arsenal or store for explosives' to possess a pack of playing cards.

LONDON HACKNEY CARRIAGE ACTS

The famous London taxis, instantly recognisable around the world, also fell under the aegis of the Metropolitan Police. Indeed, there are over thirty-seven London Hackney Carriage Acts regulating them, many of which are still in force. For example, the 1843 Act says: 'That nothing herein or in any other Hackney Act contained shall be deemed or construed to authorize any Hackney Carriage to stand or ply for Hire opposite to the General Post Office in Saint Martin's le Grand, London, or any Part thereof.' Nor were they allowed to ply for hire in or near Bloomsbury Square. And taxi drivers were not allowed to blow a horn or any other noisy instrument when plying for hire. To be a Hackney Carriage, within the meaning of the Act, the vehicle must have two or more wheels. Not only did the driver have to be licensed, so too did the waterman who watered the horses.

PLAGUES AND CORPSES

Although everyone does it, it is technically illegal to hail a cab while it is in motion. You are supposed to go to a rank or 'place appointed'. No other vehicle is allowed to park in a taxi rank and they are required to have a water trough so the horses can take a drink.

The cabby is supposed to ask every passenger if they are suffering from any 'notifiable disease such as small-pox or the plague'. As carrying suffers is illegal, he should theoretically carry out an on-the-spot medical examination, and if the passenger were to pass away during the journey, he would be committing another offence as it is also illegal for a taxi diver to carry corpses or rabid dogs. The cabby is also required to carry out a thorough search of his vehicle before allow-ing a fare to go on their way. It is his responsibility, not the passenger's, to see that nothing is left behind.

The law requiring a cabby to carry a bale of hay on the roof of his cab to feed the horse was repealed in 1976. They no longer have to carry a nose-bag on the side of the vehicle or a sack of oats. It has long since been assumed that the law requiring the cabby to carry 'adequate foodstuffs for the horse' meant a tank full of diesel.

A cabby who drives too slowly or holds up the traffic can be prosecuted for 'loitering'. One who goes too fast can be prosecuted for 'furious driving'. And whether furious or not, it is expressly forbidden for a driver to make 'insulting gestures'.

As cabbies were not allowed to leave their cabs on the public highway, the driver was allowed to urinate in public, as long as it was on the rear wheel of the vehicle with his right hand placed on it.

Quaint Courts

While policing the city, the country
and, sometimes, the rest of the world,
London established a number of
strange courts to administer some
arcane discipline of jurisprudence. The
functions of some were amalgamated
into the regular courts we know today.
Others fell by the wayside, although
they could find themselves miraculously
revived if a specific case demanded it.

THE COURT OF CHIVALRY

England's Court of Chivalry fell out of use in the eighteenth century, but after a recess of 219 years it sat again in 1954 to decide a case between Manchester Corporation and the city's Palace of Varieties. The Corporation claimed that the theatre was illegally displaying the city's coat of arms on its curtain and the theatre admitted that it had done so.

In fact, it had displayed the city's coat of arms on its curtain for over twenty years and had used it in its official seal for over sixty years without complaint. Its defence was that the Court of Chivalry had no jurisdiction in the case as the statutes governing the court, signed by Richard II in 1384 and 1389, only gave it authority to judge questions involving feats of arms. Indeed, the proceedings of the Court of Chivalry are the forerunner of all courts martial.

The plaintiffs argued that the Court of Chivalry had judged such matters since then, that using a coat of arms without permission was 'libel' and that the Court of Chivalry was the only court with the authority to adjudicate as, in matters concerning coats of arms, the civil courts had no authority – except in the case of Kingston upon Hull, whose arms had been granted by a private Act of Parliament in 1952.

Counsel for the Palace of Varieties conceded that the Court had indeed made judgements in the matter of coats of arms previously, but he argued that the court was not properly constituted without a Lord High Constable. This was an hereditary post and it had been vacant since the last holder fell foul of Cardinal Wolsey in 1521 and was executed in the Tower of London, although a surrogate is appointed for each coronation. All judgements made by the court since 1521, the defence argued, were illegal.

For this history hearing, the court sat in the College of Arms in London's Queen Victoria Street, Blackfriars, with the full panoply of heralds in tabards and officers in full-bottomed wigs. By a curious quirk, it operates under old Roman law, not the Common Law of England. But the statutes governing it were written in Norman French, which caused problems for all involved. However, Lord Goddard, sitting as surrogate for the Earl Marshall, the Duke of Norfolk, decided with impeccable logic that the court was not sitting for the first time since 1735 simply to find it had no jurisdiction or that its judgements were invalid. He found for the plaintiffs and ordered the Manchester Palace of Varieties to pay £300 costs. The case prompted some lively correspondence in the pages of *The Times*.

THE PRIZE COURT

While the Court of Chivalry had jurisdiction over arms deployed on land, the Admiralty Court maintained the rule of law at sea. According to the Admiralty, this jurisdiction was established in the reign of Edward I (1239–1307), but the first record of the court sitting occurs around 1360 in the reign of Edward III.

Originally there were three courts, one for each of the three admirals who had authority over different parts of the coastline. But a single High Court of the Admiralty was formed in the fifteenth century. It had jurisdiction over all crimes involving English ships and crews that were committed at sea. The court used the same procedures as common-law courts, but in matters concerning trade and shipping, which were by necessity more international in nature, it used Roman civil law.

In the nineteenth century, the criminal element of their work was transferred to the common-law courts, leaving the Admiralty Court jurisdiction over cases involving collisions, salvage and cargo. Eventually the Admiralty Court was merged in the High Court of Justice.

In its heyday one of the Admiralty Court's main tasks was to crack down on piracy. However, it set up a separate Prize Court which re-registered captured ships as British. This occurred at an astonishing rate, especially at the height of British sea power during the Napoleonic Wars. Between 1792 and 1812, 48,607 ships – over six million tons of shipping – that were foreign ships became British. In one year alone, the court re-registered over four thousand ships. The Admiralty Court still maintains jurisdiction over prizes, with appeal to the Judicial Committee of the Privy Council. However, the Prize Court now only sits in times of war.

THE COURT THAT DIED OF SHAME

There is another court that makes rulings on matters of heraldic distinction. This is the Earl Marshal's Court. It can trace its roots back to the Norman Conquest when the Lord Marshal sat alongside the High Constable. The word 'constable' is staple from the Saxon 'cyning staple', meaning the 'stay and hold of the King'. In Cambro-British – that is, early Welsh – it was spelt 'kwnstabl'.

The position was hereditary and continued until 1514, when Henry VIII found it so troublesome he was determined to get rid of it. At first, he declared that it had no more offices to execute, but allowed the current holder, Edward Stafford, Duke of Buckingham, to retain certain manors attached to the office. But when he was attaindered for treason in 1521 they were forfeit to the Crown. The remaining duties were apportioned to other constables, including the constable of the Tower of London.

Even before that the court had been reined in by Richard II in 1389. Its jurisdiction was restricted to 'contracts and deeds of arms' and 'things which touch war, and which cannot be discussed or determined by the Common Law'. Three years earlier, Richard had bestowed the title Earl Marshal on the then Lord Marshal, Thomas Mowbray, Earl of Nottingham. By then, he was allowed to sit alone, without the High Constable.

From 1373, the court had its own prison – the Marshalsea in Southwark, which later became a debtors' prison. As Elizabeth I refused to appoint a new High Constable, decisions of the Marshal's or Marshalsea Court could be appealed to the Queen's – or King's – Bench. But the court's men were a law unto themselves.

In 1640, the Earl Marshal's Court came under attack from the young MP Edward Hyde – later the Lord Chancellor Lord Clarendon – who denounced it as a 'tool of oppression' in his maiden speech.

He cited a number of outrageous cases. In one, a man had been ruined by a huge fine imposed by the court. His crime was that, in an argument with a boatman who had tried to overcharge him, he had called the swan on the waterman's badge a 'goose'. The court decided that, as the swan on the waterman's badge was the crest of an Earl, the defendant had insulted the upper classes and punished him severely for 'dishonouring' the crest.

In another, a tailor had enquired of a customer of 'gentle blood' – that is, he had a pedigree registered with the College of Heralds – whether he would mind awfully paying his bill. The toff, outraged by this insolence, threatened the tailor with violence. The tailor then had the temerity to point out that 'he was a good a man as his creditor'. This was taken to be an attack on the aristocracy and the tailor was hauled in front of the Earl Marshal's Court, where he was dismissed with a reprimand – provided he tear up the bill.

Hyde pointed out that, in just two days, the Earl Marshal, sitting alone, had awarded more damages than had been awarded by juries in all the actions that had been tried in all the courts in Westminster in a whole judicial term. What's more, Hyde maintained that the Earl Marshal's Court was a 'mere usurpation' that had only sprung up during the reign of Charles I and had first sat as then constituted 1633 to serve the nobility. The House of Commons agreed that, if unchecked, the court's powers might be established in law by constant usage. They never passed a bill to abolish it, but the Earl Marshal was shamed by the criticism and 'his court never presumed to sit afterwards'.

SELLING SOUTHWARK

Courts leet were manorial courts where the lord of the manor exercised jurisdiction over his tenants and bondsmen. With the end of feudalism, they went into terminal decline and many disappeared altogether. For example, Courts leet that once sat in the Southwark area of London lost their jurisdiction when the City of London bought the manors on the South Bank of the Thames from Edward VI in 1550 for £642 2s. 1d. The 'incidents' – the feudal jurisdiction – had to be purchased separately for another 500 marks. At the time a mark was worth two-thirds of a £1, so that worked out at £333 6s. 8d.

One of the few courts leet that still sits to this day, however, is the oldest court in the City of London, the Court of Husting. In the Court of Husting for Common Pleas various writs could be pleaded, including, among others, recovery of a widow's dower of lands, recovery of lands and rents, and recovery of distress wrongfully taken. Deeds and wills were also enrolled at this court, and no foreigner could be admitted into the freedom of the City of London except at the Court of Husting.

The court sat on Mondays, alternating between pleas of land and common pleas. The presiding judges were the Lord Mayor and sheriffs, or six aldermen if the Mayor was unavailable. The business of the court gradually declined and since then it has hardly been in use, its only remaining purpose being to register gifts made to the City.

IN THE COURT OF THE KING

In 1671, Colonel Thomas Blood stole the Crown Jewels from the Tower of London. He was caught red-handed and indicted for treason. The public looked forward to a big trial, followed by a bloody execution. Yet Blood not only walked free, he was rewarded. That's because he appealed to the highest court in the land – the Court of the King.

Born in Ireland in 1618, Blood came to England when the Civil War broke out, to fight for Charles I. But when it became clear that Cromwell was going to win, he changed sides. His reward was a number of estates in Ireland that had formerly belonged to the King, which he lost at the Restoration when Charles II took the throne in 1660.

With other disgruntled parliamentarians, he

attempted to seize Dublin Castle and take the governor, Lord Ormonde, prisoner. Blood then tried to free a prisoner who was on his way from the Tower of London to York for trial for treason. With a price of £100 on his head, he fled to Holland. Despite being a wanted man, he returned to England in 1670 under a false name and tried to kidnap Ormonde again.

After failing a second time – and narrowly escaping capture – he came up with a plot to steal the Crown Jewels. Following the Restoration, a new set of regalia had to be made at a cost of £12,185 – that is over £1 million today.

Blood befriended the elderly Keeper of the Jewels, Talbot Edwards. When Edwards let him see the jewels, Blood hit him on the head with a mallet and stabbed him with a sword. He flattened the crown with the mallet and shoved the orb down his breeches. Fleeing, Blood dropped the sceptre.

Regaining consciousness, Edwards cried: 'Murder! Treason!' Blood shot at one of the guards as he tried to escape, but found the iron gate locked and was arrested. As stealing the Crown Jewels constituted treason, he faced not just execution, but hanging, drawing and quartering. But Blood would say nothing to his interrogators, insisting that he would only speak to the King himself.

Charles II was intrigued so, bypassing the courts, Blood was brought before the King himself. Blood then warned His Majesty that his accomplices were still at large. If he was executed, they 'may well wreak the ultimate vengeance upon your person', he said. Then he told the King that he himself had been on a mission to assassinate him.

'Although you were at my mercy, bathing unprotected in the Thames at Battersea, the sight of Your Majesty filled me with such awe I was unable to do you any harm,' he said.

'What if I should give you your life?' said Charles, flattered.

'I would endeavour to deserve it, Sire!' Blood replied.

Blood was not only pardoned, to the disgust of Lord Ormonde, but was given Irish lands worth £500 a year! He became a familiar figure around London and made frequent appearances at court – not the sort of court that he had been trying to avoid. Plainly it pays to have friends in high places.

Edwards recovered from his wounds and was rewarded by the King. He lived to a great age, recounting the story of the theft of the jewels to visitors to the Tower.

In 1679 Blood's luck ran out. He quarrelled with his former patron the Duke of Buckingham, who demanded £10,000 over some insulting remarks Blood had made about his character. Then Blood fell ill; he died in 1680 at the age of sixty-two and the Duke never got paid.

SANCTUARY

It was possible to stay out of the way of the courts altogether by seeking sanctuary. In Anglo–Saxon times, every church had the right to shelter the fugitive from justice for seven days. However, some places offered permanent sanctuary – notably the lands around the great abbeys and churches, including Westminster Abbey and St Martin's le Grand in the City between Newgate Street and Cheapside. In 1486, Pope Innocent issued a bill relating to English sanctuaries that said anyone who left a sanctuary's asylum lost his right of protection, even if he returned later. Meanwhile, the King appointed keepers to look after those who had claimed sanctuary after being accused of treason.

Henry VIII (1509–47) withdrew the sanctuary rights of accused traitors further. Sanctuary was also denied those guilty of murder, rape, highway robbery, burglary, arson and sacrilege. Others seeking sanctuary could be brought to trial if ever they left it. All inmates had to wear a badge that was twenty by twenty inches. They were forbidden the use of weapons and could not leave their lodgings between sunrise and sunset.

James I (1603–25) abolished the right of sanctuary, apart from a few privileged places, but Charles II (1660–85) continued the process. However, the privileged places offering sanctuary in the City of London, Westminster and Southwark were only brought within regular jurisdiction in the reigns of William III (1689–1702) and George II (1727–60).

Peculiar Punishments

Those who administer the law often like to hand out bizarre punishments – sometimes they do this in a whimsical effort to make the punishment fit the crime, but at others, to our eyes at least, they seem downright barbarous.

CHEATING TRADESMEN

Dishonest tradesmen were paraded through the streets of London with a symbol of their offence. In 1517, a butcher was ordered to ride through the City of London with two sides of bacon tied to him, with two other 'flitches' carried before him, a paper attached to his head and basins being banged to attract attention 'ffor puttyng to sale of mesell [measle or diseased] and stynkyng bacon'.

For repeated convictions the offender was also sentenced to the pillory. In 1560 a crooked butcher from Theydon in Essex was 'sett in the pyllory in Cheapesyde ... with the sayd bacon hanginge about him and over his hedde uppon the saide pyllorrye, and a paper affyxed to the seyd pyllorie declarynge not only this his sayd offence, but also the like offence by him here comytted in the tyme of the mayraltye of Sir Thomas Leigh'.

Meanwhile, sellers of rotten meat in the capital are still exposed to public shame. Under Section 180 (4) of the Public Health (London) Act of 1936, anyone convicted twice of offering unfit food for sale has a 'notice of facts' affixed, not to their forehead, but to the door of their premises for twenty-one days.

FISH NECKLACE

Overcharging was considered an even graver offence, especially if the perpetrator had the temerity to overcharge the royal household. Soon after Elizabeth I came to the throne, 'one of the takers of freshe fishe for the provision of the Queenes house was set on the Pillorie in Cheape side in the fishe market over agaynst the kings head, having a bauldrike [necklace] of smeltes hanging about his necke with a paper on his foreheade, written "for buying smelts for .xij. pens a hundred, and solde them againe for ten pens a quarter'". He was to stand in the pillory for three hours on three days, then 'on the last day he should have had one of his eares slitte, if by great suyte made to the Counsayle by the Lorde Mayor of London, he hadde not beene pardoned'.

Magistrates were quite imaginative in making the punishment fit the crime. In 1478, a man convicted of illegally tapping a conduit to fill his own well was ordered to be paraded on horseback 'with a vessell like unto a conduyt full of water uppon his hede, the same water running by smale pipes oute of the same vessell and that when the water is wasted newe water to be put in the said vessell ageyn'.

In 1535 a gong farmer – or lavatory cleaner – was ordered to stand 'yn one of hys owne pypes [barrels] ... yn fylthe with a paper upon hys hed for castying of ordure yn the open stretes', while in 1551 a card sharp in Southwark got a backwards ride with 'his cote prycked full of playing cardes on every side'.

RIDING BACKWARDS

Cheating wood-sellers were ridden around with billets of wood slung around their necks and in 1553 a party of coal merchants from Edgware and Croydon were ridden around, sitting back-to-front on horseback with 'a sak of their coles hagynge aboute their neck, the one ende of the same sakkes with the one half of the coll hangynge at their bakk and thother ende with thother half of the coll hangyne on their brest'.

Back-to-front riding was a popular punishment at that time. In 1537, a minstrel was punished for keeping a woman disguised in 'mannes rayment' (men's clothes). He was ordered to ride through the city 'on horsebakke with his fact to the horse tayll with a paper on hys hedde and to play up hys owne instrument afore her'.

For slandering James I's daughter and her husband, the Elector of the Palatine and the deposed King of Bohemia, along with various other dignitaries, in 1621, Edward Floyd was sentenced to ride 'from Westminster then to the Fleete with his face to the horse tayle and the tayle in his hand, with a paper on his forehead'.

BRANDING

In November 1556, the chronicler John Stow recorded that 'a man was brought from Westminster Hall riding with his face to the horse tail, and a paper on his head, to the Standard in Cheape, and there set on the pillorie, and then burned with an hote yron on both his cheekes, with two letters "F" and "A" for False Accusing one of the court of Comon place [Common Pleas] in Westminster of treason'.

The Cheapside Standard, opposite Honey Lane, was a fountain and was rebuilt in the reign of Henry VI (1422–61). It was a traditional place of punishment. In the year 1293, three men had their right hands stricken off here for rescuing a prisoner arrested by an officer of the City. In Edward III's reign two fishmongers were beheaded at the Standard for aiding a riot. In the reign of Richard II, Wat Tyler, leader of the Peasants' Revolt in 1381, beheaded Richard Lions, a rich merchant, there. When Henry IV usurped the throne, it was at the 'Standard in Chepe' that he had Richard II's blank charters burned. In the reign of Henry VI, Jack Cade, another revolutionary, beheaded the Lord Say; the event is recalled by Shakespeare in *Henry VI, Part II*. In 1461, John Davy had his offending hand cut off at the Standard for having struck a man before the judges at Westminster.

THE CUCKING STOOL

Women were rarely sentenced to the pillory, though in late-medieval London there was a version of the pillory called the 'thew' specifically for women. By 1500, this seems to have been replaced by the cucking stool, which was designed to expose female offenders to public humiliation rather than immersion. Later, the cucking stool became the ducking stool.

In 1529, seven 'common women', probably prostitutes, were sentenced 'to be had to the cukkyng stole', though it is not clear if they were ducked. However, in 1535, a group of 'myghty vagabond and wys-women of theyre bodyes' were taken to Smithfield and 'sett upon the cukkying stooe and . . . wasshed over the eares'. By 1577,

William Harrison noted in his Description of England that 'harlots and their mates, by carting, ducking, and dooing of open penance ... are often put to rebuke'. Harrison also mentioned 'scolds' or quarrelsome women were 'ducked upon cuckingstooles in the water'.

Harsher penalties were inflicted for adultery and fornication: 'The dragging of some of them over the Thames between Lambeth and Westminster at the taile of a boat ... this was inflicted upon them by none other than the knight marshall, and that within the compasse of his jurisdiction & limits onelie' – that is, within the royal court and its environs.

This was because the cucking stool itself, in some cases, did not prove much of a deterrent. In 1566, Robert Crowley was imprisoned for stopping choirs wearing surplices – which he considered Romish – in his parishes. When a woman barracked the Bishop of London at the height of the controversy, she was 'sett uppon two laddars lyke a cuckengstole'. But this did not induce shame or repentance. Rather she 'satt the space of one owre, greatly rejoysynge in that her lewde behavowr, and that she was punyshyd for the same, and lyke wyse the beholdars of ye same dyd myche rejoyce ther in and anymatyd the lewde woman to rejoyce and prayse the Lorde for that He had made hir worthy to soffer persecution for ryght-wysnes, and for the truths sake (as they said) and for crienge owt a agaynst supersticion as they termed it'.

In fourteenth-century London, scolds or brawlers had to carry a 'dystaff with towen'. A distaff was a rod for holding flax, tow or wool while spinning and the punishment was to remind the culprits to be more womanly in their ways.

THE PUNISHMENT OF PROSTITUTES

London ordinances of the fourteenth century say that 'common women', or prostitutes, should be paraded wearing hoods made of ray – striped material – with a white wand in their hands. The parade was led through the city by minstrels, playing raucous tunes on musical instruments. Sometimes metal basins were beaten or other 'vile minstrelsy' was employed. Though for the dedicated prostitute, this surely would have constituted free advertising.

The enforced wearing of a yellow letter was used as punishment – not unlike the scarlet ones used in New England. In 1516, a prostitute was caught soliciting in priest's clothing and a bawd was convicted of procuring a thirteen-year-old girl. They were forced to parade behind banging basins, with ray hoods and carry white wands – 'the said Elizabeth Chekyn havying on her brest a letter of H, of yelowe wollen clothe in sygne and tokyn of a harlot, on her left shulder a picture of a woman in a preest goun; and the said Elizabeth Knyght havying upon her shoulder a letter of B in signe and tokyn of a bawde'.

In 1519 three common strumpets were convicted for the 'abhomynacion' of cutting their hair short like men, so that they could wear men's clothing, presumably to attract those who liked that sort of thing. They were ordered to be paraded through the streets with white wands in their hands, ray hoods about their shoulders and wearing 'mennes bonett on their hed, without eny kercher, their hed kemte' – that is, men's bonnets on their heads, without any kerchief or scarf, their heads kempt or combed.

BAD HAIR DAYS

A fourteenth-century ordinance of the City of London read: 'If any woman shall be found to be a common receiver of courtesans or bawd ... let her be openly bought, with minstrels, from prison to the thew, and set thereon for a certain time ... and there let her hair be cut round about her head'. Prostitutes suffered the same penalties for a third offence. In 1559, two 'auncyent and commen harlottes of their bodies' were to be carted through the streets with ray hoods, white wands, basins banging and the rest of it, to the pillory and 'their here to be cutt and shavyn above their eares'.

Male sexual misconduct was similarly punished: 'If any man shall be found to be a common whoremonger or bawd ... let al the head and beard be shaved except a fringe on the head, two inches in breadth; and let him be taken unto the pillory, with minstrels, and set there for a certain time'. Mind you, a haircut like that would be considered rather fashionable these days.

In 1510, the London Court of Aldermen ordered two pimps to have 'their hed to be polled [sheared or shaved]

above the eyes and the same day in markett season to
be ledde from thens to the pillorie in Cornhull thervppon
to stande by the space of an houre', while in 1561 a man
and his half-sister convicted of incest were ridden
around the City for three market days, 'havying their
heare shorne above their eares ... for a deformitie'.

PITY THE POOR

The Poor Relief Act of 7 May 1649 says that 'rogues,
vagrants, sturdy beggars, idle and disorderly persons'
found in London were to be set to work or 'duly punished
by putting in the stocks, or whipping' then to be sent
back where they came from. This was to include bastards
and other poor children. Meanwhile, any child born to
an incestuous marriage was classified as a bastard under
an Act of 1650 entitled An Act for Suppressing the
Detestable Sin of Incest, Adultery and Fornication.

PUBLIC FLOGGING

In 1780, as public sentiment turned against public flogging, it was confined to the streets outside the Old
Bailey and the Middlesex Sessions House on Clerkenwell
Green. However, a poem of the time said that 'West
End dandies paid a visit daily, To see the strumpets
whipped at the Old Bailey'. Public flogging for women
was abolished in 1817 and for men a decade later.

THE PILLORY

The pillory was introduced in Anglo–Saxon times to punish slander, using loaded dice or begging with someone else's child. Under the Normans it came to be the traditional punishment for tradesmen who had cheated their customers – particularly a butcher who sold bad meat or a greengrocer who gave short weight. It was similar to the stocks, but instead of restraining the victim's ankles, a hinged wooden frame held him by the neck and wrists. Spectators were then allowed to pelt the victim with anything that came to hand. Villains feared it more than any fine, imprisonment and even the lash. Titus Oates, the instigator of the Popish Plot of 1678, almost died from the brickbats thrown at him in the pillory.

Ears were in constant danger in the pillory. In London, in 1502, a notorious cutpurse had his right ear lopped off while he was in the pillory. That same day, the writer and publisher of seditious tales against the King and nobles was to have both his ears cut off.

More commonly, the culprits' ears were nailed to the pillory. Usually at the end of the punishment, the nails were pulled out with pincers, though in one case in London, in 1552, it was ordered that the culprit 'shall pluck it [the ear] from the pyllorie hym selfe att his goinge downe withoute the helpe of eny other or els remayne there styll'.

That same year a 'gentleman' who had had his ear nailed to the pillory in Cheapside for obtaining goods by deceit stayed in the pillory till after midnight rather than pull himself free at the risk of losing it. It did him no good as a helpful beadle 'slitted yt upwards with a penknife', freeing him.

But the threat of ear damage was usually enough. Again in 1552, a wax chandler was sentenced to spend three market days in the pillory 'for slanderous rayllyng upon my lord the mayer and his brethren th'aldermen'. But even on the pillory he protested his innocence, so he was ordered to admit his guilt publicly or suffer 'hys eares upon the rest of th'execucion of hys seid judgement to be cutt of openly upon the pyllore'. He promptly recanted and was discharged.

Under the 1562 Forgery Act, the punishment became more brutal. A convicted forger had to repay the aggrieved party double their costs and damages, was put in the pillory 'and there to have both his ears cut off, and also his nostrils to be slit and cut, and seared with irons, so as they may remain for a perpetual note or mark of his falsehood'. Then they were also to forfeit all their land and go to prison for life.

Under a statute of James I in 1623, anyone unfortunate enough to go bankrupt was nailed by one ear to the pillory for two hours, and then had the ear cut off. But in 1731, seventy-year-old forger Joseph Cook underwent the full terrible punishment while he stood in the pillory at Charing Cross.

In 1751, four men were found guilty of falsely accusing innocent people of theft for the reward money. They were so badly treated in the pillory 'that Egan was struck dead in less than half-an-hour, and Salmon was so dangerously wounded in the head that it was thought impossible for him to recover'. And in 1777, Ann Morrow, who dressed up as a man and married three different women, was 'pelted ... to such a degree, that she lost the sight of both eyes'.

The pillory was abolished as a punishment for most crimes in 1817. But until 1837, it remained the punishment for riot and perjury.

DANIEL DEFOE

Early in his career, the author of *Robinson Crusoe*, Daniel Defoe, was sentenced to the pillory. At the end of the seventeenth century, nonconformists were being driven from public life and Defoe, a dissenter, struck back with a satirical pamphlet entitled: *The Shortest-Way with the Dissenters* – meaning to kill them all – which he published anonymously. It sold well, but no one got the joke. Both dissenters and high churchmen took it seriously and were outraged when the hoax was exposed.

All too aware of the consequences, Defoe went into hiding. A few months earlier, fellow pamphleteer William Fuller had received thirty-nine lashes in Bridewell Prison, was fined one thousand marks (£666) and kept on to do hard labour until he paid it. But worse than that, he spent three days in the pillory.

'Never was a man among Turks or Barbarians known to be worse used,' said Fuller. 'I was stifled with all manner of dirt, filth and rotten eggs; and my left eye was so bruised with a stone ... that I fell down and hung by the neck ... I was all over bruised from head to heels; and on the small of my back as I stood stooping, a stone struck me which weighed more than six pounds.'

After weeks on the run, Defoe was finally arrested and charged with seditious libel. He was sent to Newgate Prison, the most dreaded of London's twenty-seven gaols. He later wrote about the experience in his book, *Moll Flanders*. His trial at the Old Bailey attracted a huge crowd, who paid a shilling a head to see Defoe in the dock.

The outcome of the trial was a foregone conclusion. The judges on the bench were men whom Defoe had lampooned in earlier pamphlets. He said that they took bribes, always favoured the rich over the poor, and at least two of them enjoyed seeing prostitutes they themselves had used being stripped and whipped in Bridewell Prison.

Found guilty, Defoe was sentenced to three days in the pillory. He could have mitigated his sentence by naming his accomplices. Instead, he wrote *Hymn to the Pillory* – another satire defaming his enemies, including the very judges who had sentenced him. It was on sale as he stood in the pillory outside the Royal Exchange on 29 July 1703, and continued to do brisk business when he stood in the pillory at Cheapside the following day and at Temple Bar on the last day of the month. His defiance was rewarded: people liked his pamphlet so much that, on all three days, he was surrounded by cheering crowds and the only things he was pelted with were flowers.

Although Defoe made money from the sale of *Hymn to the Pillory*, his judges took their revenge by detaining him in gaol until the brickworks he owned in Tilbury went bankrupt. After that, he was forced to concentrate all his energies on his literary career, so I suppose that we should be grateful to the justices.

FLEET PRISON

In 1716, there were over 60,000 people in gaol for debt in England and Wales. In most parts of the country there were no separate prisons for debtors, but in London there was a handful of them. Three of the most notorious were the Fleet, the Marshalsea and the King's Bench. The Fleet, near Blackfriars, had existed since the twelfth century and had once been a royal prison, housing those who had been convicted by the Star Chamber. It was notorious for its turnkeys, who extorted money from the inmates, often making it impossible for them to pay their debts and leave. Famous inmates included founder of the Society of Friends George Fox, founder of Pennsylvania William Penn, Richard Hogarth (William Hogarth's father) and John Cleland, who wrote *Fanny Hill* in the Fleet, where he was incarcerated for debt between 1748 and 1752. John Donne spent time there in 1602 when, at the age of twenty-nine, he contracted a secret marriage to sixteen-year-old Anne More.

Prostitution and drunkenness were rife and there were notorious Fleet marriages, often involving minors and conducted without banns or a licence by penurious priests. The Fleet was also a well-known receiving house for smuggled or stolen goods as the excise men were too afraid of the inmates to search the place.

MARSHALSEA PRISON

In 1715, the Marshalsea, on the south side of the River Thames, became home to the public hangman John Price, who lived above his means, running up debts of seven shillings and sixpence. After three years, he escaped by digging a hole through the wall. Along the way, he murdered a man, then savagely attacked and beat a woman named Elizabeth White in Bunhill Fields, Islington. She died of her injuries four days later. Price was then held in Newgate, but before he was hanged by his successor he raped a young girl who had brought food to his cell.

In 1597, dramatist Ben Jonson was held in the Marshalsea for 'Leude and mutinous behavior' on a warrant from Elizabeth I as co-author of the play *The Isle of Dogs* with Thomas Nashe. Nashe escaped. The play was suppressed and no copy exists, so it is difficult to judge how offensive it was.

The following year, Jonson was then held in Newgate after killing actor Gabriel Spenser in a duel on Hogsden [Hoxton] Fields. He pleaded guilty but was released by benefit of clergy – a legal device to escape hanging. If you would recite the fifty-first psalm – the so-called 'neck verse' – you could claim the jurisdiction of the ecclesiastical courts. His property was forfeit and he was branded on the left thumb to prevent him from claiming benefit of clergy a second time.

He returned to Marshalsea Prison for libel in 1605 with George Chapman for having offended James I with anti-Scottish references in their play, *Eastward Ho!* A report said they should have their ears and noses cut, but they were released after several months, probably because Chapman had influence at court.

THE KING'S BENCH

The King's Bench prison was nearby, off Horsemonger Lane. Writer Oliver Goldsmith and actor David Garrick visited Tobias Smollett there in 1759. The MP John Wilkes was sentenced to twenty-two months there and fined £1,000 for obscene and seditious libel. On his way from Westminster Hall to the King's Bench prison on 10 May 1768, a crowd of his supporters gathered. The Riot Act was read and the Third Regiment of Foot Guards opened fire on the mob, killing several people in what became known as the St George's Fields Massacre.

While the poor lived in appalling conditions in the prison, often for a very long time, the rich could rent an apartment, where they could live with their wives and families. The keeper of Fleet Prison charged £2 4s 6d for a room on the 'gentleman's side'. The official price was 4d.

Naturally Wilkes lived in style in the King's Bench. Friends and relations brought pork, salmon, game and wine, and paid his fines. He was also visited by his mistress, Mrs Bernard, and enjoyed the favours of other young women. In 1776, some seventy-eight prisoners lived in private houses that were actually outside the prison walls, while 241 lived inside in considerable squalor.

Prison Reform

Prison reformer John Howard complained that many debtors made a mockery of the law by living as comfortably in prison as they did at home, with no incentive whatsoever to pay their debts. Meanwhile, poorer prisoners were clapped in irons, or they were thrown into cells with prisoners suffering from smallpox or into dungeons over sewers filled with corpses.

Both the Fleet and King's Bench prisons were completely destroyed by the Gordon Riots of 1780, although they were later rebuilt. Marshalsea Prison had been moved a little to the south when Charles Dickens' father was confined there for a debt of £40 in 1824. Debtors' prisons appear in *The Pickwick Papers*, *David Copperfield* and *Little Dorrit*.

Marshalsea and Fleet prisons were closed in 1842 and the King's Bench – by then called the Queen's

Bench – became a military prison after imprisonment for civil debt was abolished in 1869. It was demolished in 1879.

NEWGATE PRISON

While traitors went to the Tower of London, ordinary criminals languished in Newgate, which existed as a prison from the 1100s to 1904, when it was finally demolished. The Old Bailey stands on the site today.

It was a hellhole. Typhus – or 'gaol fever' – killed many before the hangman got to them, and in 1414, forty prisoners and one gaoler died of gaol fever in a single week. The poor lived in absolute darkness and slept on vermin-ridden straw – they competed with the rats for the stale bread thrown to them and lice crunched underfoot as prisoners moved about. The smell was so bad that people walking by in the street would hold nosegays to their faces to cover the stench.

The better off could comfort themselves with beer and gin, which was sold by the gaolers at exorbitant prices. Pigs, pigeons and other pets could be kept in the cells up to 1792 and, until Victorian times, accommodation was mixed. In those days, trials were swift and execution or transportation occurred soon after. However, sometimes there were oversights. In 1689, Major John Bernardi was imprisoned in Newgate. Somehow his case slipped through the net and he was held there for the next forty-seven years until he died, still awaiting trial. But during that time, he and his wife and had ten children.

Burning Books

Bonfires of books and other publications condemned by the House of Commons as seditious were common until 1763. The burning was usually done by the public hangman in Palace Yard at 1 p.m. However, the Commons had such contempt for the radical John Wilkes' attack on the King's speech in issue number forty-five of the *North Briton* that they did not want to dignify it by burning it in Westminster and ordered that it be incinerated in Cheapside in the City.

When the sheriff tried to carry out the order, his officials were pelted with stones by a crowd who cried: 'Wilkes and liberty!' So the sheriff's men burned a petticoat and some jack-boots instead. Parliament was deeply disturbed by this and set up an enquiry that went on for four days. It has never attempted to burn anything ever again.

Wilkes also sued the government over his arrest. The Secretary of State, Lord Halifax, had issued a general writ, but when Wilkes noted that no one had been named, he protested that it was 'a ridiculous warrant against the whole English nation'. Nevertheless, he was locked up in the Tower of London while his papers were ransacked. He received £1,000 in compensation.

When, after being expelled from Parliament, Wilkes was elected Lord Mayor of London, the story circulated that Lord Chancellor Bathurst was attempting to exercise the royal prerogative to get him disbarred. The Lord Chancellor was present at the Royal Courts of Justice when the Mayor was sworn in and Wilkes told him: 'I am fitter for my office than you are for yours, and I must call upon the King to choose another Lord Chancellor.'

POSTHUMOUS ARREST

Just because you are dead does not mean you can escape the law. When the playwright Richard Brinsley Sheridan died, he was laid out in a friend's house in Great George Street, Westminster, where friends gathered. A man dressed in deep mourning called, saying that he had known the deceased for a long time and had come a long way in the hope of seeing his old friend one last time. With some reluctance the undertaker was persuaded to open the lid of the coffin. The man then produced a writ and a bailiff's staff, touched the corpse on the face and said: 'I arrest the corpse in the King's name for a debt of £500.'

By this time, the funeral party had arrived and, reluctant to delay the proceedings, George Canning and Lord Sidmouth wrote cheques for £250 each.

Awful Executions

One would have thought that being
put to death was punishment enough –
apparently not. In London, which
likes to see itself as one of the homes
of civilisation and justice, some
have gone to great lengths to come
up with gruesome ways of death,
both by design and accident.

BOILING ALIVE

Henry VIII was a bloodthirsty tyrant and during his thirty-eight-year reign he had more than 70,000 people executed – that's an average of more than five people a day. But he wanted something particularly gruesome to punish Richard Roose, who had been convicted of putting poison in a pot of broth intended for the Bishop of Rochester. The bishop had lost his appetite, but his guests and servants were poisoned instead.

In 1530, Henry passed a special Act. The entire wording of the untitled Act read: 'Wilful poisoning shall be adjudged high-treason, and the offender therein shall be boiled to death.'

Roose was condemned without trial and the sentence was carried out at Smithfield on 15 April 1531. According to an eyewitness: 'He roared mighty loud, and divers women who were big with child did feel sick at the sight of what they saw, and were carried away half dead; and other men and women did not seem frightened by the boiling alive, but would prefer to see the headsman at his work.'

In 1542, the cook Margaret Davy, who had poisoned her employers in three households, suffered the same terrible fate in Smithfield. After that, Edward VI passed a law, making all wilful poisoning the regular felony of murder, thereby punishable by the slightly more merciful penalty of hanging. But Henry VIII's original Act remained on the statute book until 1863.

JACK KETCH

John 'Jack' Ketch is thought to have been appointed public executioner in 1663. He was renowned for his brutal inefficiency, firstly for the botched beheading of Lord William Russell in Lincoln's Inn Fields in 1683. Having escaped being hanged, drawn and quartered, Russell refused to be blindfolded. He paid Ketch twenty guineas to do a swift job. But when the first blow of the axe glanced off the side of his neck, Russell said: 'You dog! Did I pay you to treat me so inhumanely?' It took three blows to sever the head and Ketch was jeered from the scaffold.

Two years later, Ketch took eight strokes to remove the head of James Scott, Duke of Monmouth, the eldest illegitimate son of Charles II, on Tower Hill. When Ketch was imprisoned for 'affronting' a London sheriff, a butcher named Pascha Rose was appointed in his place. A few months later Rose was arrested for robbery, after he and another man had broken into the house of a William Barnet and stolen 'a Cambler coat and other apparrel'. He was hanged at Tyburn on 28 May 1686 and Ketch was reinstated. For two centuries, Jack Ketch was the nickname of all England's executioners.

THE ETIQUETTE OF THE SCAFFOLD

Class counts, even on the scaffold. When different grades of peerage met their fate together, a duke was beheaded first, then an earl, then a baron. After the rebellion of 1745, the Earl of Kilmarnock faced execution on Tower Hill a year later and offered to let Baron Balmerino go first. But the sheriff objected, he would not let an earl go last.

Lord Capell was about to address the crowd before his execution when the executioner told him to take his hat off. This was another shocking breach of etiquette.

On another occasion a chimney sweep and a highwayman were being taken to Tyburn on the same cart. Travelling up Holborn Hill, the highwayman said to the sweep: 'Stand off, fellow.'

The sweep retorted: 'Stand off yourself, Mr Highwayman; I have as good a right to be here as you have.'

PRESSING

Under the Statute of Westminster of 1275 those who refused to plead or who challenged more than twenty prospective jurors were to be starved into submission. But in 1406 *peine forte et dure* – the strong and hard punishment – was introduced. Unless the accused pleaded guilty or not guilty, they were chained to the ground and weights were piled on top of them until they chose to talk or their internal organs burst and they died. This was used so frequently that Newgate had a special yard set aside for pressing.

The wording of the judgement was:

That the prisoner shall be remanded to the place from whence he came, and put in some low, dark room, and that he shall lie without any litter or other thing under him, and without any manner of garment, except something to hide his privy member; that one arm shall be drawn to one quarter of the room with a cord and the other to another, and that his feet shall be used in the same manner; and that as many weights shall be laid upon him as he can bear, and more; that he shall have three morsels of barley bread a day, and that he shall have the water next to the prison, so that it be not current; and that he shall not eat the same day on which he drinks, not drink on the same day on which he eats; and that he shall continue so till he die or answer.

Men would undergo this terrible ordeal if they stood to be convicted of a crime that would mean their titles and property would be forfeit to the Crown. If they died under the *peine forte et dure* they would secure their possessions for their heirs.

In 1712, Thomas Cross and William Spigot were ordered to be pressed to death at the Old Bailey. On seeing the preparations being made, Cross gave in and pleaded. But Spigot was made of sterner stuff. His sufferings are described in *The Annals of Newgate*:

The chaplain found him lying in the vault upon the bare ground with 350 pounds weight upon his breast, and then prayed by him, and at several times asked him why he would hazard his soul by such obstinate kind of self-murder. But all the answer he made was – 'Pray for me, pray for me!' He sometimes lay silent under the pressure, as if insensible to pain, and then again would fetch his breath very quick and short. Several times he complained that they had laid a cruel weight upon his face, though it was covered with nothing but a thin cloth, which was afterwards removed; yet he still complained of the prodigious weight on his face, which might be caused by the blood being forced up thither, and pressing the veins as violently as if the forced had been externally upon his face. When he had remained for half-an-hour under this load, and 50 pounds weight more laid on, being in all 400 pounds, he told those who attended him he would plead. The weights were at once taken off, the cords cut asunder; he was raised by two men, some brandy was put in his mouth to revive him, and he was carried to take his trial.

Peine forte et dure was not used in treason cases, as standing mute was considered a guilty plea. Last used in 1741, it was abolished in 1772 and an Act of 1827 said that a 'not guilty' plea was to be recorded for anyone refusing to plead.

HANGING, DRAWING AND QUARTERING

The dreaded punishment of hanging, drawing and quartering was only abolished on 4 July 1870, although it had long fallen into disuse. The victim was strung up by the neck and partially hanged, then castrated and disembowelled while they were still alive. Their entrails were burnt in front of their faces, then their body was cut into four. This terrible punishment was inflicted because, in a time when life was nasty, brutish and short, to be despatched swiftly with a blow of the axe was no deterrent.

Originally the body was cut into four quarters so that the pieces could be taken to the four corners of the country to demonstrate the fate of traitors. Later the flesh was distributed around Temple Bar, the City Gates and the Tower of London.

On 13 October 1660, Samuel Pepys wrote: 'I went out to Charing Cross to see Major-General Harrison' – one of the regicides – 'hanged, drawn and quartered, which was done there, he was looking as cheerful as any man could do in that condition. He was presently cut down, and his head and heart shown to the people, at which there was great shouts of joy.'

On 20 October, he wrote: 'This afternoon going through London and called at Crowe's, the upholster's in St Bartholomew's, I saw the limbs of some of our new traitors set upon Aldersgate, which was a sad sight to see; and a bloody week this and the last have been, there being ten hanged, drawn and quartered.'

The practice of displaying the severed head on a pike on top of the Tower of London or on London Bridge was ended in the 1700s. The last people to be beheaded were the Cato Street conspirators, who planned to assassinate the Cabinet in 1820. They were 'drawn', too, but not by having their entrails drawn out of them. Rather they were drawn to the scaffold on a hurdle – a rectangular frame or sled.

THE GIBBET

Gibbets were erected on all the roads into London at Kensington, Knightsbridge, Hampstead, Highgate, Finchley, Wimbledon and Putney. Bodies were left there to rot as a warning to others and to slow the process they were covered with tar. However, this made it easy for friends and relatives of the culprits to set fire to the corpse.

The gibbet was frequently the fate of captured pirates brought to London for trial and execution. Pirates, smugglers and mutineers who were condemned to death by the Admiralty courts were taken to Execution Dock on the Thames at Wapping, where they were hanged at the low tide mark, as the Admiralty courts writ only ran at sea. They were left hanging there while three tides passed over their heads. Their bodies were hung in chains at Cuckold's Point or Blackwall Point on the Thames as a warning to other seafarers.

Captain Kidd was found guilty of piracy and being hanged in chains was the penalty. The sentence was carried out at Execution Dock, just downstream of the Tower of London, on 23 May 1701. The first rope broke and he had to be strung up a second time. A heavy man, he would have died quickly. After the tide had washed over him three times, he was painted in tar, bound in chains and put in a metal harness that would keep his skeleton intact while his flesh rotted away. The body was then displayed hanging from a gibbet that cost £10 to build at Tilbury Point, where anyone sailing in or out of the Thames could see it. His remains hung there for three years.

There were objections that these displays in the lower reaches of the Thames offended foreign visitors of London and did not uphold the majesty of the law, though the scenes even became gruesome tourist attractions. Samuel Pepys expressed disgust and the practice was formally abolished in 1834.

THE ANATOMY ACTS

Henry VIII had signed an Act allowing the Company of Barber-Surgeons the bodies of four executed felons each year and Elizabeth I extended the privilege to the College of Physicians, who also got four. However, the demand for fresh corpses made a ready market for grave-robbers, who were known as 'sack-'em-up' men. Then in 1752 an Act for better preventing the horrid crime of murder was passed, which required that the bodies of all hanged murderers should be delivered to Surgeons' Hall. The idea was that the law should add a further deterrent as most people then believed that you could not be resurrected into the afterlife if you were not buried intact. But this still did not stop the trade in corpses.

In 1831, John Bishop, James May and Thomas Williams tried to sell the corpse of a fourteen-year-old boy to Guy's Hospital. It was refused. They tried again at the King's College School of Anatomy in the Strand, asking for nine guineas, but Richard Partridge, the demonstrator of anatomy, spotted the body was fresh. There were no signs that it had been buried and there was a cut on the forehead. They were delayed by Partridge, who said he had to get change for a £50 note, and they were arrested. Bishop's home in Nova Scotia Gardens, Bethnal Green, was searched and clothing found, suggesting multiple murders.

Bishop and Williams admitted other murders and selling the victims' bodies for dissection. They were hanged at Newgate, thereby providing the anatomists with a couple of much-needed corpses, and their remains displayed. The crime scene at Nova Scotia Gardens was opened by the police, with an admission charge of five shillings. The third of the so-called London Burkers – after the notorious Burke and Hare in Edinburgh three years earlier – James May was transported to Australia as it was thought he had no knowledge of the murders. He died on the voyage.

As a result of the public outcry, the 1832 Anatomy Act was passed. This allowed any corpse to be legally dissected, provided its owner had not expressly objected while alive. It put the sack-'em-up men out of business.

BONFIRE NIGHT

Some culprits deserved to be punished long after they were dead, or so it was thought – one such was Guy Fawkes. On 5 November 1605, he was caught trying to blow up the King and the Houses of Parliament in the ill-fated Gunpowder Plot. The conspirators were arraigned in Westminster Hall and seven were taken from the Tower to the Star Chamber by barge. Another, who was considered lower class, was brought from the Gatehouse Prison, which was built into the gatehouse of Westminster Abbey. They were found guilty of high treason and hanged, drawn and quartered in St Paul's churchyard. Two other plotters who had been killed resisting arrest were dug up, decapitated and their heads exhibited on spikes outside the House of Lords.

Even that was not enough. Later that year, the Observance of 5th November Act was passed, which required the people of England to celebrate 'with unfeigned thankfulness ... this joyful day of deliverance' as a 'perpetual remembrance ... for all ages to age to come'. That did not mean you had to build a bonfire, burn old Guy in effigy and set off fireworks. Instead you were supposed to go to church, where prayers of thanksgiving were to be said 'and there to abide orderly and soberly at the time of the said prayers, preaching or other service of God'. No more burnt jacket potatoes at the end of the back garden, then. The law making it compulsory to celebrate the arrest of Guy Fawkes stayed in force in England and its Dominions until 1859.

However, one law concerning Bonfire Night still seems to be in force. Its says it is only permissible for children to go door to door collecting 'a penny for the Guy' with the written permission of the local chief constable of police. Whether kids are allowed to 'trick or treat' on Halloween without the chief constable's consent is a moot point.

PUNISHED POST-MORTEM

After the Restoration of the Stuart king in 1660, the corpse of Oliver Cromwell was exhumed from its resting place in Westminster Abbey and taken to Tyburn, where it was hung up in chains beside those of the other regicides. His body was then thrown in a pit beneath the gallows and his head was stuck on a pole on the top of Westminster Hall, where it remained until the end of the reign of Charles II.

Much the same fate befell a Roman Catholic banker named Stayle. He was a victim of the so-called Popish Plot, an outburst of anti-Catholic hysteria in 1678. Finding him guilty of treason, the Lord Chief Justice Sir William Scroggs said: 'Now you may die a Roman Catholic and when you come to die, I doubt you will be found a priest too. The matter, manner, and all the circumstances of the case make it plain. You may harden your heart as much as you will, and lift up your eyes, but you seem instead of being sorrowful to be obstinate. Between God and your conscience be it; I have nothing to do with that; my duty is only to pronounce judgment upon you according to law. You shall be drawn to the place of execution, where you shall be hanged by the neck, cut down alive . . .'

After this terrible sentence had been carried out, Scroggs heard that Stayle's friends had said a mass for him. He then ordered the body to be taken out of the grave, and the quarters fixed on the gates of the City, and the head on a pole on London Bridge. It was said of Scroggs: 'He was so proud of his exploit that he caused an account of the case to be published by authority.'

Stayles was, of course, entirely innocent.

ALL THE LAW ENTRAILS

In 1694, a gentleman named Walcott was executed as a traitor. Along with the usual hanging, drawing and quartering, he received an attainder, which meant that all his property – both real, as in land, and personal – was forfeit to the Crown and his blood was said to be corrupt, which meant that no title could be passed on to his heirs.

His son sought to have this overturned on the grounds that, when the sentence of hanging, drawing and quartering was passed, the judge omitted the bit about the prisoner's entrails being burnt in front of his face. The Crown argued that the hanging, drawing and quartering was the substantive part of the judgement and the bit about burning the entrails was only added *in terrorem* – to frighten. In any case, it was 'inconsistent in nature for man to be living after his entrails were taken out of his body'.

Nevertheless, the King's Bench found in the son's favour. It said that it found it extraordinary that the Crown could argue that 'judgement in high treason was discretionary, which is indeed only a softer word for arbitrary'. The judgement continued: 'If that doctrine should once pass for law, then the Courts which give judgements might make new punishments as they should think more suitable to the crimes; they might pronounce a Jewish judgement, "that the offender should be stoned to death"; or a Turkish judgement, "that he should be strangled"; or a Roman judgement, "that he should be murdered"; or a French judgement, "that he should be broken on a wheel"; all which are contrary to the known laws of this realm. This being then an essential part of the judgement settled and stated by common law of England, the omission of these words makes it void.'

The King's Bench also said that 'judges are like the officers of the Mint, who must not vary from the standard, either in weight or fineness'. The Crown's contention that sentence could not be carried out – as the condemned man would be dead when his entrails were removed – was dismissed as it was to 'arraign the wisdom and knowledge of all the judges and King's Counsel in all reigns' and the son's counsel pointed to the case of Colonel Harrison, one of Charles I's regicides, who 'was cut down alive, and after his entrails were taken out of his body rose up, and had strength enough left to strike the executioner'.

The case went all the way to the House of Lords, who upheld the King's Bench's decision. By varying the words, the sentence was illegal. Sadly this was little consolation for Walcott Senior. Whether his entrails were in fact burnt in front of his face and whether, like Colonel Harrison, he survived that much of the ordeal is not recorded, but the attainder was lifted and the son's blood uncorrupted, allowing him to inherit.

Tyburn Tomfoolery

The traditional place for executions
was Tyburn, where Marble Arch
now stands, although there were also
gallows in Soho Square, Bloomsbury
Square, Smithfield, St Giles in Holborn,
Blackheath, Kennington Common and
on City Road in Islington. Occasionally
people were publicly hanged outside
the place where they had committed
a particularly heinous crime.

TREE OF JUSTICE

The place of execution was then known as Tyburn Fields, which was a large area of rough ground through which the River Ty flowed – 'burn' meaning river or stream in Old English. A stand of elms grew on the banks of the Ty and the Normans considered the elm to be the 'tree of justice'. At least fifty thousand people died a violent death at Tyburn between 1196 and 1783, when executions there ended.

Tyburn was well situated and the open ground meant that huge crowds could congregate to watch the spectacle. It was also on the main roads into London from the north and the west, and so hangings there acted as a deterrent to those heading into the City. The elm trunks were later used as conduits to carry fresh water from the Ty into the City.

LONGBEARD

The first person to be executed at Tyburn was William 'Longbeard' Fitzrobert in 1196. He led a rebellion against the tax being levied to ransom Richard the Lionheart from Henry VI of Austria. When the rebellion failed, William sought sanctuary in St Mary-le-Bow in the City of London, but the Archbishop of Canterbury, Hubert de Burgh, who was also Chief Justiciar of the Kingdom (prime minister and chief justice rolled into one) ordered his men to set fire to the church to force

Longbeard out. De Burgh later sought sanctuary himself. When this proved controversial, to say the least, de Burgh fled to Wales.

SINGLE BEAM

The Middlesex Gallows were built on the west of the stream and featured a single beam where ten prisoners could be hanged at one time. The condemned criminal would be made to climb a ladder and the hangman would attach the noose to the beam before 'turning off' the felon so they swung free. Once the horse and cart was introduced to transport the victims from Newgate, it was used in the execution, too. The felons would stand on the cart with their hands tied behind their backs and once all their necks were secured to the beam, the hangman would pull a cap down over the prisoner's face and whack the horse on the flanks. It would take off, taking the cart with it and leaving the condemned criminals swinging. After half an hour, the bodies were cut down.

THE TRIPLE TREE

The first permanent gallows were built at Tyburn in 1571. The single beam was replaced with a 'triple tree' – a gallows with three beams, which could each accommodate eight people, so the executioner could hang twenty-four people at a time. During the reign of

James I, around 150 people were hanged a year. By the 1700s, up to forty a day were being despatched, with Tyburn fairs held every six weeks.

FOR WHOM THE BELL TOLLS

The condemned criminals were held in the Tower of London if they were of high rank. Otherwise they languished in the filthy dungeons of Newgate Prison. London merchant Robert Dow, a leading member of the Worshipful Company of the Merchant Taylors, left an annuity to pay for a man to ring a handbell twelve times outside the condemned cell in Newgate at midnight before an execution, ensuring the occupants had no sleep, reminding them of their imminent death and urging them to repent. He believed it would help the condemned prepared themselves for their journey to the next world. The condemned were also subjected to a hellfire-and-damnation sermon in a chapel hung in black with their coffins on a table in front of them, while the rest of the congregation gawped on.

Initially criminals were dragged behind a horse from Newgate to Tyburn, but this often led to their premature death, depriving the crowds at Tyburn of the spectacle they had turned out to see. Later they were dragged on an ox skin or a sled, but it was eventually found more sensible to bring them from Newgate by cart, which could also carry their coffins and the pastor to comfort them on the way.

Notorious criminals often dressed up for the occasion as if going to a wedding and would be cheered by the crowds. The first stop was the Church of St Sepulchre, where the bell was tolled twelve and they were given a bunch of posies. The bell at St Sepulchre's would sound again once the execution was completed. A pigeon released at Tyburn would carry the news back. The tolling of the bell was also paid for by Robert Dow's annuity of a modest one pound, six shillings and eight pence – or £185 at today's prices. The practice was ended with the hanging of Mary Pearcey on 23 December 1890. A guest at the Viaduct Hotel near St Sepulchre's fell ill and the vicar was asked to suspend the bell ringing. As the procession to Tyburn had ended more than a century before, the tradition was never renewed.

The sexton of St Sepulchre's, who reached the condemned cell via a tunnel under the road, also recited a verse that read:

All you that in the condemned hole do lie,
Prepare you for tomorrow you shall die;
Watch all and pray: the hour is drawing near
That you before the Almighty must appear;
Examine well yourselves in time repent,
That you may not to eternal flames be sent.
And when St Sepulchre's Bell in the morning tolls
The Lord above have mercy on your soul.

Which must have been a comfort. This verse now appears on the stand of the Newgate Execution Bell, which is kept in St Sepulche-without-Newgate at Holborn Viaduct.

ONE FOR THE ROAD

The condemned were taken in procession to Tyburn. At the hospital of Church of St Giles-in-the-Fields the condemned were given a jug of ale and they stopped at every pub on the way, most famously at the White Hart on Drury Lane. Each publican would give them free ale, as the condemned men and women would bring in the crowds. This is the origin of the expression 'one for the road'. One Captain Stafford on his way to the gallows asked for a bottle of wine. He had an urgent appointment to keep, he said, but would pay for it on the way back. It is said that one teetotaller refused refreshment and was hanged moments before a messenger with a reprieve arrived on horseback – had he stopped for a drink he would have been saved. The tradition of stopping for drinks on the way was ended in 1750, though a pub named the Bowl was built on the site of St Giles' Hospital.

CARNIVAL

Hampered by huge crowds, the procession along Oxford Road, now Oxford Street, could take hours. Popular prisoners were showered with flowers, while unpopular ones were pelted with rotten vegetables and stones. The whole thing had a carnival atmosphere with the crowds singing and chanting, and street vendors selling gingerbread, gin and oranges.

Around the gallows there were wooden stands, where spectators paid two shillings for a good view. The largest stand with the best view was Mother Proctor's Pews, after Mother Proctor who owned it. On one occasion – the execution of an earl – she made £500. But things could go awry. In 1798, pew owner Mammy Douglas jacked up her prices for the hanging of the traitor Dr Henesey. The public duly paid up. But when Henesey was given a last-minute reprieve, there was a riot. The stands were demolished and Mammy Douglas narrowly escaped replacing Henesey on the scaffold.

'OH MY, THINK I'VE GOT TO DIE'

When the cart carrying the condemned arrived, there would be cries of 'Hats off!' and 'Down in front!' so everyone got a good view. Bawdy songs were sung along with, as well as a revivalist hymn that carried the line: 'Oh my, think I've got to die'.

A priest would say a prayer and the condemned were invited to publicly confess their crimes. Some gave long speeches in self-justification; others seized the moment to abuse the authorities, the hangman, the priest or the crowd. The smuggler John Biggs told the crowd: 'I never was a murderer, unless killing fleas and suchlike harmless little cruelties fall under the statute. Neither am I guilty of being a whore-master, since females have always had the ascendancy over me, not I over them. No, I am come here to swing like a pendulum for endeavouring to be too rich, too soon.'

'LAUGHING JACK' HOOPER

Things were rarely as dignified at Tyburn as they were at the Tower. One hangman, 'Laughing Jack' Hooper, who officiated at Tyburn from 1728 to 1735, was renowned for clowning about on the scaffold.

Jack Ketch, who was as bad a hangman as he was an axeman, was told by condemned man James Turner: 'What, dost thou intend to choke me? Pray fellow, give me more rope! What a simple fellow is this. How long have you been executioner that you know not where to put the knot?'

As the cap was being pulled down over his face, Turner spotted a pretty girl in the crowd and blew her a kiss. And as the rope tightened, he said: 'Your servant, mistress.'

Another felon with an eye for the ladies was Tom Austin. When asked by the chaplain if he had anything to say before he hanged, he said: 'Nothing, only there's a woman yonder with some curds and whey. I wish I could have a pennyworth of them before I'm hanged 'cos I don't know when I'll see any again.'

STRIPPED FOR ACTION

The hangman was entitled to keep the victims' clothes. Latterly these were taken after the hanged felon was cut down, before the body was sent to the anatomist. But in 1447, five men were stripped ready for hanging when their pardons came through. The hangman refused to return their clothes and they had to walk home naked.

Hannah Dagoe, an Irish girl who robbed a friend in Covent Garden in 1763, put on quite a show. In Newgate she terrorised her fellow prisoners and stabbed a man who had given evidence against her. In the cart on the way to Tyburn, she paid no attention to the Catholic priest with her. Under the gallows she got her hands free and punched the hangman so violently she knocked him down. Then she dared him to hang her. As it was plain that this was exactly what it was that he was going to do, she decided to take her revenge on him by giving away her clothes. She stripped off her hat, cloak and dress and threw them into the crowd. The hangman struggled to get the noose around her neck. But as soon as he had done so, she threw herself off the cart with such violence that she broke her neck and died instantly.

DISPOSING OF THE BODY

The bodies also belonged to the hangman. Although he was obliged to sell those of murderers to surgeons for dissection, he sometimes sold them back to their families, if they offered a better price. Sometimes it was difficult to keep the corpse intact as the crowd would grab bits of it as a souvenir. On 18 December 1758, there was a riot when the medics fought the family for possession of a body. The mob won and carried the corpse away in triumph. The hangman would also cut up the rope and sell bits of it in the pubs in Fleet Street.

HANGING ABOUT

Sometimes felons were hanged near to where the crime took place. On 21 January 1664, Samuel Pepys recorded in his Diary:

> Up, and after sending my wife to my aunt Wight's, to get a place to see Turner hanged, I to the 'Change'; and seeing people flock to the City, I enquired, and found that Turner was not yet hanged. So I went among them to Leadenhall Street, at the end of Lyme Street, near where the robbery was done; and to St. Mary Axe, where he lived. And there I got for a shilling to stand upon the wheel of a cart, in great pain, above an hour before the execution was done; he delaying the time by long discourses and prayers, one after another in hopes of a reprieve; but none came, and at last he was flung off the ladder in his cloak. A comely-looking man he was, and kept his countenance to the end; I was sorry to see him. It was believed there were at least 12,000 to 14,000 in the street.

Triple murderer Sarah Malcolm was hanged in Fleet Street between Fetter Lane and Mitre Court, nearby where she had murdered her mistress and two fellow servants. The twenty-two-year-old showed no contrition and when the bellman came to Newgate threw him a shilling to buy wine. At her execution, though, she acted with dignity and resignation. She fainted and was, with difficulty, revived.

'Oh, my mistress, my mistress,' she said. 'I wish I could see her.'

As the cart pulled away she commended her soul to Christ. 'Laughing Jack' Hooper was affected by this; either he believed she was innocent or had been touched by the newspaper stories about her fall from grace and quit soon after. John Thrift took over as hangman, despatching thirteen on his first day as executioner without so much as a titter.

THE MOVING GALLOWS

By 1759, the Tyburn gallows were beginning to impede traffic on its way in and out of London, so the triple tree was demolished and a 'moving gallows' was used. Timbers from the old gallows were sold to local pubs as barrel stands, though some were retained by the Tyburn Convent as relics of Catholics who had been martyred there. Later a toll gate was installed at the site, which proved more unpopular than the gallows.

A New Method of Hanging

On 5 May 1760, Laurence Shirley, the fourth Earl Ferrers was executed at Tyburn. A drunk and violent man, he had quarrelled with the agent who ran his estates and shot him dead. He was imprisoned in the Tower of London and tried by the House of Lords in Westminster Hall. Found guilty, he asked to be beheaded on Tower Hill, but their lordships decided that he should be hanged like a common criminal at Tyburn and then given to the anatomists to be dissected. He asked to be hanged with a silken cord, instead of a hemp rope, as befitted his rank. This, too, was denied. However, the novel introduction at his hanging would be the use of a trapdoor. A platform had been raised about eighteen inches above the scaffold with a hatch about three feet square in it. The Earl would stand on it and put the noose put around his neck. Then the hatch would open, killing him. At least that was the theory.

For his execution, Ferrers wore the white suit trimmed with silver that he had worn on his wedding day. He travelled from the Tower to Tyburn in his own landau and six. The crowds were so thick that it took nearly three hours.

'They have never seen a lord hanged before,' he remarked to the sheriff.

The procession comprised a detachment of Grenadier Guards, a company of Life Guards, lines of constables, numerous City officials, coaches full of friends and well-wishers, and a hearse. No one wanted to miss the spectacle. The Earl, nonchalantly chewing tobacco, waved to the crowds. And when the horse of a dragoon escorting him got its leg caught in the wheel of the coach and threw his rider, Ferrers remarked: 'I hope there will be no death today but mine.'

According to Horace Walpole, the cortège 'was stopped at the gallows by a vast crowd, but [he] got out of his coach as soon as he could, and was but seven minutes on the scaffold, which was hung with black . . . The mob was decent, admired him, and almost pitied him.'

What unpleasantness there was took place on the scaffold. After handing his watch to the sheriff and five guineas to the chaplain, Ferrers mistakenly gave another five guineas to the assistant hangman, rather than the headman, Thomas Turlis, himself. The two men came to blows. Eventually the sheriff stepped in and gave the money to Turlis.

The Earl did get some privileges due to his status. He had his hands tied in front of him with a black sash, rather behind him with ordinary cord. Turlis then guided him on to the raised part of the scaffold, which was covered with black baize.

'Am I right?' asked the Earl.

Turlis nodded and pulled the white cap down over his face. Then he operated the mechanism and Ferrers dropped. But there had been a grave miscalculation.

'As the machine was new, they were not ready at it,' said Horace Walpole. 'His toes still touched the stage and he suffered a little, having had time, by their bungling to raise his cap; but the executioner pulled it down again, and they pulled his legs so that he was soon out of pain, and quite dead in four minutes.'

After an hour the body was taken down. This resulted in another brawl between the hangmen.

'The executioners fought for the rope,' said Walpole, 'and the one who lost it, cried.' The rope, of course, was valuable.

The body was then laid in a coffin lined with white satin and taken to Surgeons' Hall, where it was cut open and put on display for the next three days, before being handed over to his family for burial.

Turlis also had squabbles with the condemned. On 27 March 1771, he was hanging five men at Tyburn when he was struck in the face during an altercation and was injured. Five days later, on his way back from a hanging at Kingston in Surrey, he collapsed in the cart and died.

FATHER AND SON

The job of hangman was taken over by Edward Dennis. But when the anti-Catholic Gordon Riots – instigated by the fanatical protestant Lord George Gordon – broke out, Dennis was seen smashing up a chandler's shop. He was arrested in the Blue Posts pub in Southampton Buildings, Holborn, and charged with being one of the riots' ringleaders. At his trial Dennis broke down and begged for mercy. Nevertheless, he was sentenced to death. However, as his death would plunge his family into penury he asked that his son succeed him as executioner. The newspapers made great play out of the fact that the father was going to be hanged by the son. In the event, the authorities had a problem. Fifty-nine rioters had been condemned, but they had nowhere to hold them as the rioters had burnt down Newgate Prison. Dennis's talents were needed and he was reprieved so that he could hang his fellow rioters.

Now that the Tyburn gallows were mobile, Dennis could do his work in the City at Bishopsgate, in Bow Street and in Bloomsbury Square, as well as at Whitechapel, Oxford Road and Old Street. It is thought he officiated at the hanging of three rioters – William McDonald, Mary Roberts and Charlotte Gardiner – on Tower Hill, making them the last people to be executed there.

Too Posh to Swing

By the end of the eighteenth century, the area around Tyburn was beginning to get built up. Mayfair became a posh residential district and even the traditional May Fair was banished to Fairfield in Bow, in the East End, in 1764 and the new residents were none too pleased to have regular Tyburn fairs on their doorsteps.

In 1771, the Dowager Lady Waldegrave began building a grand house nearby and the newspapers reported that 'through the particular interest of her Ladyship, the place of execution will be moved to another spot'. There were objections that public executions drew too many spectators.

'Sir, executions are intended to draw spectators,' said Dr Johnson. 'If they do not draw spectators, they don't answer their purpose.'

On 7 November 1783, John Austin became the last man to be hanged at Tyburn. Convicted of robbery and wounding, he was despatched by the old horse-and-cart method. Again the execution was bungled: the knot slipped around the back of Austin's neck, prolonging his death.

After that Tyburn Lane became Park Lane, Tyburn Road became part of Oxford Street and Tyburn Gate became Cumberland Gate. Meanwhile, the home of public hanging in London became the street outside the newly rebuilt Newgate Prison in the Old Bailey.

HANGING'S NEW HOME

After 1783, executions were restricted to Newgate and Horsemonger Lane in Southwark, where they were still a popular entertainment. Edward Dennis and his assistant William Brunskill performed their first executions outside Newgate on 9 December 1783. Their new mobile gallows were kept in a shed in Newgate and hauled out with horses when needed.

The gallows were eight feet wide and ten feet long with two parallel cross beams that could carry ten criminals – and there was room for City officials to sit. They also featured the trap system, which had not developed much from the one used unsuccessfully on Earl Ferrers. The ten despatched that day strangled slowly as the ropes used were much too short. This was not rectified for another ninety years; it was only then, behind closed doors, that the bodyweight to rope length ratio required to snap the neck cleanly was worked out. Until then, it was considered better for a felon to strangle slowly at the end of a short rope, rather than use a long rope which risked tearing the head off and showering the spectators with blood.

At it was, the local residents were not pleased with the new venue. A newspaper reported: 'The inhabitants of the neighbourhood, having petitioned the sheriffs to remove the scene of the execution to the old place, were told that the plan had been well considered, and would be persevered in.'

The truth was that the residents of the posh houses growing up around Hyde Park held more sway. The regular processions from Newgate to Tyburn disrupted trade in a newly built-up shopping area and the wild Tyburn fairs held along one of the main thoroughfares of London gave visitors a bad impression. Far fewer spectators could fit into the area around the Old Bailey so the crowds were easier to control. And the residents soon got used to the idea when they began renting out rooms with windows overlooking the scaffold every time there was a hanging. By 1840 it cost £25 – over £15,000 at today's prices – to rent a window with a good view,

and the keeper of Newgate would entertain distinguished guests with a lavish breakfast of devilled
kidneys and brandy on execution days.

ACCIDENT PRONE

Three years after the gallows had been moved to
Newgate, Dennis died in his apartment in the Old Bailey
and Brunskill took over. At his first solo performance –
hanging seven before a large crowd – he took a bow.
However, Brunskill became a little accident prone. On
5 June 1797, he was executing Martin Clench and James
Mackley, who claimed to be innocent of the murder of
Sydney Fryer. As Brunskill and his assistant John
Langley were about to pull down their caps, the trapdoor gave way and the two condemned men along with
their executioners and priests tumbled down the hatch.
The felons were stopped abruptly by the ropes, while
the others landed in a heap at the bottom.

A Newgate hanging went even more disastrously
wrong on 22 February 1807 when John Holloway and
Owen Haggerty went to the scaffold still protesting that
they were innocent of the murder of John Cole Steel
on Hounslow Heath five years before. They were joined
by Elizabeth Godfrey, who had been convicted of the
wilful murder of Richard Prince the previous Christmas
by stabbing him in the eye with a pocket knife. Together,
they were hanged at about a quarter past eight.

According to the Newgate Calendar:

The crowd which assembled to witness this execution was unparalleled, being, according to the best calculation, nearly forty thousand; and the fatal catastrophe which happened in consequence will for long cause the day to be remembered. By eight o'clock not an inch of ground was unoccupied in view of the platform. The pressure of the crowd was such that, before the malefactors appeared, numbers of persons were crying out in vain to escape from it; the attempt only tended to increase the confusion. Several females of low stature who had been so imprudent as to venture among the mob were in a dismal situation; their cries were dreadful. Some who could be no longer supported by the men were suffered to fall, and were trampled to death. This also was the case with several men and boys. In all parts there were continued cries of 'Murder! Murder!' particularly from the females and children among the spectators, some of whom were seen expiring without the possibility of obtaining the least assistance, everyone being employed in endeavours to preserve his own life.

The most affecting scene of distress was seen at Green Arbour Lane, nearly opposite the debtors' door. The terrible occurrence which took place near this spot was attributed to the circumstance of two piemen attending there to dispose of their pies. One of them having had his basket overthrown, which stood upon a sort of stool with four legs, some of the mob, not being aware of what had happened, and at the same time being severely pressed, fell over the basket and the man at the moment he was picking it up, together with its contents. Those who once fell were never more suffered to rise, such was the violence of the mob.

At this fatal place a man of the name of Herrington was thrown down, who had by the hand his youngest son, a fine boy about twelve years of age. The youth was soon trampled to death; the father recovered, though much bruised, and was amongst the wounded in St Bartholomew's Hospital. A woman who was so imprudent as to bring with her a child at the breast was one of the number killed. Whilst in the act of falling she forced the child into the arms of the man nearest to her, requesting him, for God's sake, to save its life. The man, finding it required all his exertion to preserve himself, threw the infant from him, but it was fortunately caught at a distance by another man, who, finding it difficult to ensure its safety or his own, got rid of it in a similar way. The child was again caught by a man, who contrived to struggle with it to a cart, under which he deposited it until the danger was over, and the mob had dispersed. In other parts the pressure was so great that a horrible scene of confusion ensued, and seven persons lost their lives by suffocation alone. It was shocking to behold a large body of the crowd, as one convulsive struggle for life, fight with the most savage fury with each other; the consequence was that the weakest, particularly the women, fell a

sacrifice. A cart which was overloaded with spectators broke down, and some of the persons who fell
from the vehicle were trampled underfoot, and never
recovered. During the hour that the malefactors
hung, little assistance could be afforded to the
unhappy sufferers; but after the bodies were cut
down, and the gallows removed to the Old Bailey
Yard, the marshals and constables cleared the street
where the catastrophe occurred, and, shocking to
relate, there lay nearly one hundred persons dead,
or in a state of insensibility, strewed round the street!
Twenty-seven dead bodies were taken to St
Bartholomew's Hospital, four to St Sepulchre's
Church, one to the Swan, on Snow Hill, one to a
public-house opposite St Andrew's Church, Holborn;
one, an apprentice, to his master's; Mr Broadwood,
pianoforte maker, to Golden Square. A mother was
seen carrying away the body of her dead boy; Mr
Harrison, a respectable gentleman, was taken to his
house at Holloway. There was a sailor-boy killed
opposite Newgate by suffocation; he carried a small
bag, in which he had some bread and cheese, and
was supposed to have come some distance to behold
the execution. After the dead, dying and wounded
were carried away, there was a cartload of shoes,
hats, petticoats and other articles of wearing apparel
picked up. Until four o'clock in the afternoon most
of the surrounding houses had some person in a
wounded state; they were afterwards taken away by
their friends on shutters, or in hackney-coaches. The

doors of St Bartholomew's Hospital were closed against the populace. After the bodies of the dead were stripped and washed they were ranged round a ward on the first floor, on the women's side; they were placed on the floor with sheets over them, and their clothes put as pillows under their heads; their faces were uncovered. There was a rail along the centre of the room: the persons who were admitted to see the shocking spectacle went up on one side of the rail, and returned on the other. Until two o'clock the entrances to the hospital were beset with mothers weeping for sons, wives for their husbands and sisters for their brothers, and various individuals for their relatives and friends.

The next day (Tuesday) a coroner's inquest sat in St Bartholomew's Hospital, and other places where the bodies were, on the remains of the sufferers. Several witnesses were examined with respect to the circumstances of the accident, which examination continued till Friday, when the verdict was, 'That the several persons came by their death from compression and suffocation'.

Paper Hanging

One morning in the spring of 1818, the artist George Cruikshank, who illustrated many of the books of Charles Dickens, was strolling in the City when he came across the gallows still hanging with corpses. Two of the bodies belonged to young women who looked barely older than sixteen. When he asked a bystander what the girls had done, he was told that they been hanged for trying to forge a £1 note.

Shocked, Cruikshank drew his own £1 note with a row of corpses hanging from a gallows where the head of Queen Victoria should be. When his drawing was published it caused outrage. The Bank of England even had to stop issuing £1 notes for a time and, under public pressure, the Home Secretary Sir Robert Peel was forced to abolish the death penalty for minor crimes in 1832.

GRUESOME SCENE

Despite the horrors, the law still allowed public executions. On 2 January 1827, a bookseller in Holborn named Charles Thomas White was found guilty of attempting to burn down his own house for the insurance and was sentenced to death. On the scaffold he struggled violently with the hangman James Foxen and his assistant, Thomas Cheshire. When Foxen moved to operate the drop, White got his hands free and wrenched off his cap. As the drop fell, he jumped up and grabbed hold of the rope. An eyewitness said:

> During his exertions his tongue had been forced from his mouth, and the convulsions of his body and the contortions of his face were truly appalling. The cries from the crowd were of a frightful description, and

they continued until the executioner had forced the wretched man's hand from the rope and, having removed his feet from the platform, had suffered his whole weight to be sustained by the rope.

The distortions of his countenance could even now be seen by the crowd, and as he remained suspended with his face uncovered, the spectacle was terrific. The hangman at length terminated his sufferings by hanging on to his legs, and the unhappy wretch was seen to struggle no more.

HORRORS OF THE GIBBET

Following the example of Cruickshank, Charles Dickens lent his weight to the campaign to end public hanging. After seeing the execution of Maria and Frederick Mannings for murdering her lover Patrick O'Connor in Horsemonger Lane outside the Surrey County Gaol on 13 November 1849, he wrote to *The Times* saying:

I believe that a sight so inconceivably awful as the wickedness and levity of the immense crowd collected at that execution this morning could be imagined by no man, and could be presented in no heathen land under the sun. The horrors of the gibbet and of the crime which brought these wretched murderers to it faded in my mind before the atrocious bearing, looks and language of the assembled spectators. I came upon the scene at midnight ... As the night

went on, screeching and laughing, and yelling in
strong chorus of parodies on Negro melodies, with
substitutions of 'Mrs. Manning' for 'Susannah' and
the like were added to these. When the day dawned,
thieves, low prostitutes, ruffians and vagabonds of
every kind, flocked on the ground, with every variety
of offensive and foul behaviour ... When the sun
rose brightly it gilded thousands upon thousands of
upturned faces, so inexpressibly odious in their
brutal mirth or callousness that a man had cause to
feel ashamed of the shape he wore. When these two
miserable creatures who attracted all this ghastly
sight about them were turned quivering into the air
there was no more emotion, no more pity, no more
thought that two immortal souls had gone to judgement, than if the name of Christ had never been
heard in this world.

Although it was a degrading spectacle – Mrs Manning
fainted while being pinioned and had to be revived with
brandy – according to *The Times* the two 'died almost
without a struggle'. And in the event, the crowd, who
had been so raucous the night before, were well behaved
too: 'Scarcely a hat or a cap was raised while the drop
fell; and the bodies of the murderers had hardly ceased
to oscillate with the momentum of their fall before the
spectators were hurrying from the scene.'

Final Spectacle

Public hangings were ended in 1868 and the last took place outside Newgate on 26 May that year. The man hanged was an Irish terrorist called Michael Barrett who had blown up the Clerkenwell House of Detention, killing six people. Again, a drunken crowd stayed up all night to see the execution and they cheered wildly when the scaffold was brought out at dawn. Then more people – mainly young women and children – began to arrive. By the time a bell sounded at eight o'clock announcing the arrival of the condemned man, the crowd stretched back as far as Smithfield.

According to *The Times*:

> With the first sound of the bells came a great hungry roar from the crowd outside, and a loud, contained shout of 'Hats off', till the whole dense, bareheaded mass stood white and ghastly-looking in the morning sun, and the pressure on the barriers increased so that the girls and women in the front rank began to scream and struggle to get free. Amid such a scene as this and before such a dense crowd of white faces, Barrett mounted the steps with the most perfect firmness. This may seem a stereotyped phrase, but it really means that more than is generally imagined. To ascend the ladder with one's arms and hands closely pinioned would be at all times difficult, but to climb a ladder to go to a certain death might try the nerves of the boldest.

Final Spectacle

Barrett walked up coolly and boldly. His face was as white as marble, but still he bore himself with firmness, and his demeanour was as far removed from bravado as from fear. We would not dwell on these details, but from the singular reception he met as he came upon the scaffold. There was a partial burst of cheers, which was instantly accompanied by loud hisses, and so it remained for some seconds, till as the last moment approached the roars dwindled down to a dead silence. To neither cheers nor hisses did the culprit make the slightest recognition. He seemed only attentive to what the priest was saying to him, and to be engaged in fervent prayer.

The hangman instantly put the cap over his face and the rope round his neck. Then Barrett turning spoke through his cap and asked for the rope to be altered, which the hangman did. In another moment Barrett was a dead man. After the bolt was drawn and the drop fell with a loud boom which always echoes from it, Barrett never moved. He died without a struggle. It is worthy of remark that a great cry rose from the crowd as the culprit fell – a cry which was neither an exclamation or a scream, but it partook of the sound of both. With the fall of the drop the crowd began to disperse, but an immense mass waited till the time for cutting down came, and when nine o'clock struck there were loud calls of 'Come on, body snatcher!' 'Take away the man you've killed!' etc. The hangman appeared and cut down the body amid a storm of yells and execrations as has seldom been heard even from such a crowd. There was nothing more to be seen, so the concourse broke up with its usual concomitants of assault and robbery.

ODD OFFENCES

A comprehensive statute of 1722 made it a capital offence for 'being disguised within the Mint'; damaging Westminster and other bridges; impersonating out-pensioners of Greenwich Hospital; or being seen in the company of gypsies. By 1800 there were some two hundred capital offences on the statute books.

In the 1750s, two-thirds of those convicted in London and Middlesex were actually hanged. But as transportation and being confined to the hulks came in, that number dropped below one-third.

The age of criminal responsibility was seven and children were routinely executed. In 1814, on one day alone five children aged between eight and fourteen were sentenced to death in the Old Bailey alone. In 1833, a nine-year-old boy was sentenced to death for stealing paint worth tuppence h'apenny from a shop, while a twelve-year-old was transported for seven years for stealing two penny rolls and a thirteen-year-old was transported for life after taking a companion's hat when they were watching a puppet show.

THE SHORT DROP

The old-fashioned method of hanging used at Tyburn was the 'short drop' of just three or four feet. The hangmen used a noose with a running knot which tightened around the felon's neck, strangling them. Their writhing, apparently, provided more entertainment. It would take thirty minutes or more to die, and friends and relatives would often pull on the victim's feet to hasten the process.

Once the felon had been hanged, women would rush forward and press their face or breasts to the still-twitching hands, as this was thought to cure blemishes. They would also hold up infants, as the sweat of a dead criminal was thought to be beneficial. Lengths of hangman's rope and shavings from the gallows were also thought to have a curative effect.

THE LONG DROP

The improved 'long drop' method that instantly broke the victim's neck when they fell through a trapdoor was introduced when public hangings moved to Newgate in 1783, but it did not take over completely.

William Calcraft, the official executioner for the City of London and Middlesex from 1829 until 1874, still favoured the short-drop method and would hang on to his victim's legs if he thought their death was coming too slowly. His successor William Marwood re-introduced the long-drop method, where the victim fell six to ten feet, breaking their neck instantly. It was turned into a precise science by James Berry, who took over as executioner in 1883 and developed a formula involving the weight, height, build, age and state of health of the person to be despatched. He calculated that an eleven-stone man needed a drop of nine feet, a twelve-stone man needed eight feet eight inches, while a fourteen-stone man needed just eight feet, and adjusted the rope accordingly.

In 1886 a House of Lords committee on executions laid down the procedure which was used up until the abolition of the death penalty in 1965. But this still allowed for some individual initiative. According to the last hangman Albert Pierrepoint, the positioning of the knot was crucial. It had to force the victim's head back sharply as they fell, both breaking their neck and rupturing the jugular vein so that death came instantaneously.

HALF-HANGED SMITH

Some victims preferred the short-drop method as it offered some hope of salvation. After serving time as a sailor and a soldier, John Smith, the son of a farmer from Malton in Yorkshire, settled in London, where he became a housebreaker. He was arrested and arraigned on four indictments for stealing shoes, cloth, China silk and gloves on 5 December 1705. These were capital offences. Tried at the Old Bailey, he was convicted on two counts and sentenced to death, but the Newgate Calendar says, 'he seemed very little affected with his situation, absolutely depending on a reprieve, through the interest of his friends'.

Nevertheless, on Christmas Eve he was transported from Newgate to Tyburn to be hanged, using the short-drop method. Smith had been hanging there for nearly fifteen minutes and life appeared to have been extinguished when a reprieve arrived. He was quickly cut down and taken to a pub where he was bled – and revived.

Returned to Newgate Prison, he became a star as 'Half-hanged Smith'. People flocked to see him and he published an account of his hanging.

When I was turned off (hung) I was sensible of very great pain, occasioned by the weight of my body, and felt my spirits in a strange commotion, violently pressing upwards. These having forced their way into my head I saw, as it were, a great blaze or glaring light, which seemed to go out of my eyes – and then I lost all sense of pain. I saw my soul rising upwards into the ether – then I was cut down and began to come to myself, the soul returning the blood and spirits forcing themselves into their former channels, put me, by a sort of pricking or shooting to such intolerable pain that I could have wished those hanged who had cut me down.

On 20 February 1706, Smith was pardoned, but he had not learnt his lesson. He ran a pub in Southwark, but in January 1706 he was picked up near Fenchurch Street after breaking into a warehouse. After eighteen months in Newgate, he was acquitted on a technicality.

He was indicted again in 1720. This time the prosecutor died before the day of the trial and he was released again. Arrested again the following year, he spent more time in Newgate, but it was only in 1727 that London rid itself of Half-hanged Smith. At the age of sixty-six – twenty-two years after his hanging – he was transported to the American colonies.

In England if a condemned man survived three attempts to hang him, the sentence was automatically commuted to life imprisonment. The most famous case was that of John Henry George Lee – also known as 'Babbacombe Lee' – a footman who was found guilty of murdering his employer, elderly spinster Emma Ann Whitehead Keyse, who had been found hacked to death in the burnt-out remains of the villa in Babbacombe, South Devon, in 1884. Although the executioner tested the trapdoor, with Lee on it, it did not open.

Released in 1907, still protesting his innocence, he toured the country as 'The Man They Could Not Hang' and a silent film was made about his life. What happened to him subsequently is a matter of conjecture. According to one theory, he emigrated to America in 1917, where he married and lived on until 1933. The rock band Fairport Convention released an album called *'Babbacombe' Lee* in 1971.

Une capture.

Odd Acts

All sorts of oddities get swept up into
the law. Legislators particularly love to
pass Acts about sex, but they get carried
away about other things, too. Acts that
seemed sensible at the time, with the
hindsight of history, often appear less so.

METROSEXUAL

In an effort to cut down on 'molly houses' – homosexual brothels – in London in the sixteenth century, it became illegal for two adult men to have sex in the same house as a third person. Men were prohibited by sixteenth-century law from sampling the dubious pleasures of 'a buttered bun' – that is, having sex with a woman who had just had sex with one or more other men.

The buggery of 'mankind or beast' was outlawed by Henry VIII in the Buggery Act of 1533. The Act was repealed in 1553 on the accession of Queen Mary, but it was re-enacted by Queen Elizabeth I in 1563. The punishment was death by hanging, unless you were posh. In that case you were afforded the privilege of beheading. Although the Act was repealed again by the Offenses Against the Person Act 1828, buggery remained a capital offence under its provisions until 1861.

Curiously, Oscar Wilde fell foul of 'an Act to make further provision for the Protection of Women and Girls, the suppression of brothels, and other purposes' of 1885. As far as we know, in Oscar's case there were no women or girls involved. Neither were other men. Oscar and Lord Alfred Douglas were sharing underage boys. An amendment to the Act outlawed acts of 'gross indecency' between two men, though it had the discretion not to spell out what gross indecency meant.

According to an old city ordinance, it is against the law to check into a hotel in London under assumed names for the purpose of lovemaking. The fine for 'falsifying a hotel registration' to obtain a room for sex rather than sleeping is £20. It is also illegal to make love in trains, buses, parked cars, churchyards, churches or parks.

This is sadly at odds with the teachings of the good book, or one edition of it at least. In 1631, an authorised edition of the Bible was printed in London with a key 'not' missing. This turned the stern seventh commandment into the exhortation: 'Thou shalt commit adultery'. Its printers, Robert Barker and Martin Lucas, were fined £3,000 and the so-called 'Wicked Bible' became a much sought-after item.

PROSTITUTION

Although prostitution is legal, in London it is illegal to 'patronise a prostitute'. The penalty is a fifteen-day gaol term and a substantial fine. Prostitutes are not allowed to walk the streets and 'publicly solicit or sell' their wares. And men soliciting sex from a strange woman in public also risk a three-month gaol sentence and a fine. This law was designed to prevent men crudely propositioning any attractive woman they might meet on the street. However, in another legal loophole, it is OK for a man to proposition another man and gay prostitutes are free to solicit partners for paid-for sex sessions.

In an effort to curb prostitution in London massage parlours, it was made illegal to take money for touching another person's genitals in such establishments. If sexual services are being offered, the officer must then search the premises for schoolchildren. According to the Children and Young Persons Act of 1933 it is against the law for children and 'yowling persons' between the ages of four and sixteen to set foot in a brothel.

BERMONDSEY MARKET

The antiques market in Bermondsey traditionally set up at 4 a.m. This was because it worked under *marché ouvert* – or 'open market' – rules introduced in 1189. These rules were also known as the 'Thieves Charter'. An early form of consumer protection, they maintained that anything bought from a stallholder between sunrise and sunset was the legal property of the buyer – even if it turned out that it had been stolen. So the stalls in Bermondsey needed to be ready to open as soon as the sun was up. The idea was that respectable citizens would be unlikely to be up at that hour. *Marché ouvert* rules were abolished by the Sale of Goods (Amendment) Act 1994.

IMPERSONATING A CHELSEA PENSIONER

It is illegal to impersonate a Chelsea Pensioner. It is generally thought that this law was enacted to prevent conmen stealing the pensions of these kindly old gentlemen; but they are not so innocent. The Chelsea and

Kilmainham Hospitals Act of 1826, which offers this protection, also allows the hospital commissioners to kick out any pensioner 'convicted of a felony or misdemeanour, or who shall in any way misconduct himself'. Kilmainham Hospital was the Irish equivalent of the Chelsea Hospital when England and Ireland were still united.

Plainly both hospitals were having trouble with the old rascals at the time. Another provision of the Act required all linen at these veterans' homes to be stamped with the name of the hospital to stop the pensioners nicking the sheets. The Act made it specifically illegal for 'any pensioner or other person or persons [to] unlawfully pawn, sell, embezzle, secrete or dispose of, or for any pawnbroker or other person or persons [to] unlawfully take in pawn, buy, exchange or receive any clothes, linen, stores or other goods or articles marked, stamped or branded as aforesaid'. This law is still in force, so you'd better be on your best behaviour, you old rogues!

PROBLEMS WITH PRECEDENCE

Occasionally problems with precedence arise. These are usually settled by the chief of staff to the Lord Chamberlain without reference to the Court of Chivalry, which had jurisdiction over the matter but had not sat for over two hundred years. One such problem arose in 1953 when there was a re-organisation of the royal household and it was decided that the coroner to the royal household, whose job it is to hold inquests on anyone who dies within the precinct of a royal palace, should be moved from the medical household, where he was inappropriately lodged – as he clearly showed up the shortcomings of the other members – into the royal household proper.

The position of the coroner to the royal household is an ancient one. He is appointed by the Lord Steward of the household and is paid the princely sum of £24 from the civil list. The Coroners Act of 1887 requires him to live in a royal residence, unless the Lord Steward considers that it is more convenient for him to reside elsewhere. The problem was that the precedence of the coroner to the royal household had never been established within the royal household itself. Where should he be placed? Was he, for example, more important than the master of the Queen's music? Should he come before or after the young son of a Lord of Appeal in Ordinary or a Knight Bachelor? Wherever he came, it would be controversial as he would shift all those following him down one notch in precedence.

A high-level meeting of officials of the royal household was called in the Lord Chamberlain's office in St James's Palace, the senior royal palace in Cleveland Row. The case was outlined with all its complex nuances. Lieutenant-Colonel Sir Terence Nugent, GCVO, chief of staff to the Lord Chamberlain, then pronounced judgement. The coroner to the royal household would come after the poet laureate, but before the royal barge-master. Sir George Titman, OBE, MVO, then secretary to the Lord Chamberlain's office, obediently wrote this down. No one questioned the decision and no reason was given, but there the coroner remains.

CYCLING

After the introduction of the safety bike in 1885, cycling became a craze in England. But it soon presented problems on the roads. Cyclists speeding past horse-drawn vehicles frightened the animals and often led to angry encounters. In the historic county of Middlesex, which incorporates London north of the Thames, the local authority passed a ruling that cyclists should either dismount when a horse-drawn vehicle approached or, if they wanted to pass, they should 'inquire politely of the carriage driver for permission to overtake'.

BUMBOATS

In 1762 the delightfully named Bumboat Act was passed. Bumboats were originally boats permitted under Trinity House Bye Laws of 1685 to remove the 'filth' from ships lying at anchor in the Pool of London, but they soon began selling fruit, vegetables and other provisions to the ships. The 1762 Act aimed to regulate this trade, which must have been unsavoury if not unhygienic. As a result, the Thames police were founded and the bumboats had to be registered and numbered.

LONG TITLE ACTS

In English law there is such a thing as a Short Title Act. This is not one of them. The title of the 1750 Act regulating pilotage on the Thames, among other things, reads: 'An Act to continue several Laws for the better regulation of Pilots, for the conducting of Ships and Vessels from Dover, Deal and Isle of Thanet up the Rivers of Thames and Medway; and for the permitting of Rum or Spirits of the British Sugar Plantations to be landed before the Duties of Excise are paid thereon; and to continue and amend an Act for preventing Frauds and Admeasurements of Coals with the City and Liberty of Westminster, and several Parishes near thereunto; and to continue several Laws for preventing Exactions of Occupiers of Locks and Weirs upon the River Thames Westward; and for ascertaining the Rates of Water Carriage upon the said River, and for the better Regulation and Government of Seamen in the Merchants Service; and also to amend so much of an Act made in the first Year of the Reign of King George the First, as relates to the better Preservation of Salmon in the River Ribble; and to regulate Fees in Trials at the Assizes, and Nisi Prius ["unless before" – meaning a civil trial held before judge and jury], upon Records issuing out of the Office of Pleas of the Court of the Exchequer; and for the apprehending of Persons in any County or Place, upon Warrants granted by Justices of the Peace in any other County or Place; and to repeal so much of an Act made in the twelfth Year of the Reign of King

Charles the Second, as relates to Time during which the Office of Excise is to be kept open each Day, and to appoint for how long Time the same shall be kept open upon each Day for the future; and to prevent the stealing and destroying of Turnips; and to amend an Act made in the second Year of his present Majesty, for better Regulation of Attornies and Solicitors'.

It is surprising how often turnips turn up in English law.

THE VAGRANCY ACT OF 1824

Under this Act you can be convicted of being 'an idle and disorderly person, or a rogue, vagabond, or incorrigible rogue'. It also outlaws people 'professing to tell fortunes' including 'palmistry'. Under this Act, it is an offence merely to be suspected. The punishment was one month in a house of correction.

VENUS VICTRIX

The laws against obscenity sprang from London courts. In 1727, at the King's Bench, bookseller Edmund Curll was tried for printing and marketing a translation of *Vénus dans le Cloître* (*Venus in the Cloister*) and *A Treatise of the Use of Flogging in Venereal Affairs*. The books were condemned because they 'tend to disturb the civil order of society'. Curll was fined and sentenced to an hour in the pillory at Charing Cross. Clearly the public did not disapprove of his literary ventures. 'At the end of the hour, during which nothing more actually occurred,' wrote a witness, 'Curll was hoisted up on the shoulders of a couple of his strongest supporters and taken off to a nearby pub for a few pints.' The first Obscene Publications Act was not passed until 1857.

A BILL OF PAINS AND PENALTIES

If the divorce of Prince Charles and Princess Diana caused a scandal, it was nothing compared to the divorce proceedings of George IV and Queen Caroline, which resulted in fifty-two days of detailed testimony before the House of Lords in 1820. And it was but one incident in the scandalous life of one of the most hated monarchs ever to sit on the British throne. When George was crowned at the age of fifty, the poet Leigh Hunt wrote in *The Examiner* that the new king was 'a violator of his word, a libertine head over heels in debt and disgrace, the companion of gamblers and demi-reps ... and a man who has just closed half a century without one single claim on the gratitude of his country or the respect of posterity'. Hunt was fined £500 and jailed for two years for libel. Under English law, speaking the truth is no defence. Telling the truth is still considered libel if it is done maliciously, or even seditiously.

George IV began his scandalous sex life with one of his mother's maids of honour when he was sixteen.

Queen Charlotte admonished the boy for keeping 'improper company' in his rooms after bedtime. Taking his mother's advice to heart, he began an affair with actress Mary Robinson, who came to his apartments dressed as a boy. The Prince promised her £21,000 on her twenty-first birthday for services rendered. It was one of many debts he did not pay, so when they broke up she threatened to publish a number of highly charged letters he had sent her. To prevent a scandal, his father, George III, had to recover them. It cost him £5,000, plus a pension of £500 a year.

Soon after, wealthy divorcée Mrs Grace Elliott claimed that the Prince of Wales was the father of her daughter, whom she named Georgina in his honour, although she had been entertaining two other men at the time. Besides society ladies, George scythed his way through maids, cooks, prostitutes and actresses. At eighteen, another scandal befell the Prince when he fell for the 'divinely pretty' Countess von Hardenberg, wife of the ambassador of Hanover. When her husband read about it in the *Morning Herald*, he wrote a curt note to the Prince. The Countess wrote, too, begging him to elope with her. Unsure what to do, the Prince confided in his mother, who cried a lot. His father expelled the Hanoverian ambassador and again admonished his son for bringing shame on the family.

A born troublemaker, the Prince teamed up with the radical politician Charles James Fox – whose future wife he had already seduced – to oppose his father's policies in Parliament. Otherwise he continued his career as a playboy and got into drunken brawls in the notorious Vauxhall pleasure gardens. The King complained that there was something bad about him in the newspapers every day. Even *The Times*, a pillar of the establishment, described him as a man who 'preferred a girl and a bottle to politics and a sermon'.

At the age of twenty-three, the Prince fell in love with Mrs Maria Fitzherbert and tried to kill himself when she refused his advances. When that failed, he threatened to abdicate so he could emigrate with her to the newly independent United States of America. But she would only entertain his propositions when he promised to marry her.

Not only was she twice divorced, but any marriage between them was quite illegal. In an effort to curb the excesses of this offspring, George III had passed the Royal Marriages Act in 1772, which prevented members of the royal family under the age of twenty-five marrying without the sovereign's consent. And he was not about to give it. Even if he had consented, Mrs Fitzherbert was a Catholic, so marrying her was also illegal under the Act of Settlement of 1701. She was also six years older than him and a commoner. But in 1785 the Prince of Wales went ahead and married her anyway.

Even the way the ceremony was carried out was scandalous. George paid £500 to get an Anglican priest out of debtors' prison and he agreed to marry them on the promise of a bishopric. For political reasons Mrs Fitzherbert was sworn to secrecy, but George himself failed to be discreet. He set up home with 'Princess Fitz' quite openly in Park Street, Mayfair, and she bore him ten children.

If that was not scandalous enough, when drunk, he would attack her – more than once, she had to flee from his unsheathed sword – and he was constantly unfaithful to her.

A fresh scandal erupted when Lucy Howard bore him an illegitimate child. He paid £10,000 and a fine selection of jewellery to bed Anna Crouch, star of John Gay's West End hit *The Beggar's Opera*. Her husband, a naval officer, demanded another £400 not to drag him through the divorce courts. George also left them a sheaf of passionate love letters, which assured him a healthy income for many years to come.

He began a very public affair with Frances Villiers, Countess of Jersey, who was forty and a grandmother nine times over. There was a problem, though: he could not afford both Lady Jersey and Mrs Fitzherbert on the £50,000 a year his father gave him. Although this was considered a fortune at the time, his stables alone cost him £31,000 a year and his gambling debts were legendary.

By 1791, his debts topped £630,000. He was now in the embarrassing position of being refused credit and Mrs Fitzherbert, once a wealthy woman, had to pawn her jewellery to stave off the bailiffs.

George III and the Prime Minister William Pitt the Younger struck a deal. The government would settle the Prince's debts, provided he married and gave the country a much-needed heir. The pretty, intelligent,

Louise of Mecklenburg-Strelitz was their favoured candidate. But Lady Jersey considered her too formidable a sexual rival, so the Prince plumped instead for the short, fat, ugly and smelly Princess Caroline of Brunswick. She was considered 'excessively loose' even by German standards and a distinct odour followed in her wake, even though the British envoy sent to Germany to bring her to England persuaded her to wash herself and her underwear before they left.

Whatever charms she might have possessed were hidden beneath the unflattering gowns and heavy make-up that Lady Jersey, who had somehow inveigled herself into the position of Caroline's lady of the bedchamber, persuaded her to wear. When the Prince first saw her, he said: 'Pray, fetch me a glass of brandy. I am unwell.'

For the next three days up to the wedding ceremony, he continued consuming brandy at an alarming rate. On the morning of the wedding, he sent his brother to tell Mrs Fitzherbert that she was the only woman he had ever loved. That did not stop him leering drunkenly at Lady Jersey throughout the ceremony.

On the wedding night he was so drunk that he slept with his head in the fireplace. The following morning, he did his duty, though. To everyone's surprise, Caroline gave birth to a daughter, Princess Charlotte, nine months later. The honeymoon was a surprisingly passionate affair though, but only because George had the foresight to take Lady Jersey along.

With the birth of Princess Charlotte, George considered that he had fulfilled his side of the bargain he had made with Parliament and he told Caroline that he had no intention of sleeping with her ever again. When the news broke, the public were overwhelmingly on the Princess's side. When George went out, mobs howled: 'Where's your wife?'

The scandal also affected the palace and the King was forced to take a hand.

'You seem to look on your union with the Princess as merely of a private nature,' he wrote, 'and totally put out of sight that as Heir Apparent to the Crown your marriage is a public act, wherein the kingdom is concerned.'

The Prince of Wales tried to smooth things over. He wrote to the Princess, explaining that 'our inclinations are not in our power'. He also reminded her of the importance of 'being polite'. Caroline asked the politician George Canning what George meant by 'being polite'. Canning said that George was giving her permission to sleep with whomever she wanted, provided she was discreet. Caroline immediately took advantage of this edict and promptly slept with George Canning.

For his part, George dumped Lady Jersey and crawled back to his 'real and true love' Mrs Fitzherbert. She received him coldly. In an attempt to worm his way back into her affections, George lost some of his considerable girth and began spending freely on his London home Carlton House and his Pavilion in Brighton, even though the Napoleonic Wars were putting a considerable strain on the public purse. Mrs Fitzherbert eventually took him back into her bed when the Pope sent confirmation that, in the eyes of the Church, she was the true wife of the Prince of Wales.

Of course, it was too much to expect him to be faithful. He sired a string of illegitimate children and slept with a number of French women, even though Britain and France were at war at the time. Mrs Fitzherbert, who was now in her middle age, accepted that he chased after pretty young women, but she was more than a little distressed when he sought out a series of grand-mothers. When Napoleon heard that George was in love with the old and overweight Lady Hertford, he laughed uproariously.

In November 1810, George III became permanently insane and the Prince of Wales took over as Prince Regent. A king in all but name, he dismissed Mrs Fitzherbert coldly with the words: 'Madam, you have no place.'

This was no indication that he was taking his new responsibilities seriously. Mrs Fitzherbert and Lady Hertford had been dumped in favour of the portly Lady Bessborough, whom he begged to 'live with him publicly'. Her husband was made Lord Chamberlain and their son was also found a position in the royal household.

By this time the public were so used to George's excesses that such scandalous behaviour ceased to shock. However, new scandal was about to arrive from an unexpected quarter.

After the breakdown of the royal marriage, Caroline of Brunswick had moved to Blackheath, now in south-east London. There, according to Lady Hester Stanhope, she had become 'a downright whore' and she was frequency 'closeted with young men'. In her front room, she had a Chinese clockwork figure that, when you wound it up, made gross sexual movements and she liked to dance around showing off a good deal of her body.

Her partner in crime was Lady Douglas, who had been shunned by polite society for having an affair with her husband's commanding officer, Sir Sidney Smith. Not only did Lady Douglas take lovers whenever she felt like it, she also slept with Caroline.

When the two of them fell out, Caroline sent Lady Douglas's husband, Sir John Douglas, an obscene drawing showing his wife making love to Sir Sidney Smith. Rumours flew that a four-year-old boy in their circle named William Austin was her illegitimate son by Prince Louis Ferdinand of Prussia. This caused such a scandal that Parliament set up a Royal Commission to investigate the Princess of Wales' behaviour. It was called the 'Delicate Investigation'.

The commission investigated every sordid detail of the goings-on in Blackheath. Of particular public interest was her relationship with Captain Manby, a naval officer who was a frequent visitor. However, on the substantive charge that she had an illegitimate child, Caroline was exonerated and Lady Douglas, who had started the rumour, was found guilty of perjury.

While the Delicate Investigation was supposed to be held in secret, it proved impossible to prevent the details being leaked to the press, who printed up every sordid detail.

In 1814, Caroline left England and started a scandalous progress across Europe. She began by dancing topless at a ball in Geneva, which had been given in her honour. In Naples, she had an affair with Napoleon's brother-in-law's King Joachim. And in Milan, she took up with Bartolomeo Pergami, a former quartermaster in Napoleon's Italian army. They travelled around Europe, North Africa and the Middle East together as man and wife, before setting up home in Como, Italy.

With her own reputation in tatters, Caroline tried to ruin her daughter's, too. Charlotte had been strictly brought up by her maiden aunts in Windsor, but when she visited her mother, Caroline locked the young virgin in a room with Captain Hesse, who was said to be the illegitimate son of the Duke of York and one of Caroline's own lovers.

George III eventually died in 1820 and the Prince Regent came to the throne as George IV. He offered Caroline £50,000 a year if she promised to remain abroad, but she saw herself as Queen of England and was determined to be crowned in Westminster Abbey alongside her husband.

She returned to England and was immediately arrested and arraigned before the House of Lords for 'a most unbecoming and degrading intimacy with a foreigner of low station' – Pergami. A Bill of Pains and Penalties was drawn up, which, George hoped, when it was enacted would deny Caroline her title of queen consort and dissolve their marriage on the grounds of adultery.

The debate in the House of Lords went into the most lascivious detail. Witnesses were called, including servants from Caroline's own household, who said they had seen Caroline and Pergami naked together. Pergami had been seen caressing Caroline's breasts and her inner thigh; they slept together; he was frequently seen naked, or semi-naked in her bedroom; and he was present when she took a bath. It seemed an open-and-shut case.

The public lapped up every juicy detail. But people also knew what the King had been up to. What was sauce for the goose was sauce for the gander, was the consensus. When the Duke of Wellington was stopped by a mob who shouted 'God Save the Queen', he replied: 'Well, gentlemen, since you will have it so. God Save the Queen – and may all your wives be like her.'

Caroline herself found that she was cheered by crowds when she travelled from her new home in Hammersmith to the Palace of Westminster to listen to the proceedings. The crowds of her supporters grew so huge that a stout timber fence had to be built around the House of Lords. The proceedings reached a climax when she was called to testify. When asked whether she had ever committed adultery, she said only when she slept with 'Mrs Fitzherbert's husband'.

The hearings went on for fifty-two days and the bill was passed with a majority of just nine. But the matter had become a cause célèbre. To save the government from any further embarrassment, the bill was discreetly dropped, rather than taken forward to the House of

Commons, as there was little prospect of it being passed. Summing up the situation, one contemporary satirist wrote:

> Most gracious Queen we thee implore
> To go away and sin no more;
> Or if that effort be too great
> Go away at any rate.

But she was not about to. She was looking forward to the coronation, which was scheduled for 19 July 1821. Caroline wrote to the Prime Minister, Lord Liverpool, asking what she should wear. He wrote back saying that she could 'form no part of the ceremony'.

She turned up anyway, dressed in a sheer muslin slip and accompanied by a large contingent of supporters. Arriving at the doors of Westminster Abbey, she shouted: 'Open for the Queen. I am the Queen of England.'

The pages did as they were bid, but a courtier bellowed to the guards: 'Do your duty. Shut the door.'

The doors were slammed in Caroline's face. Undaunted, she sent the King a note asking for her coronation to be organised for the following Monday.

When news reached England of Napoleon's death on 5 May, George was told simply that his greatest enemy was dead. He replied: 'Is she, by God.'

Caroline did die, just three weeks after George IV was crowned. It was so convenient and a popular conspiracy theory of the time was that she had been poisoned. The King, it was noted, was 'gayer than might be proper to tell'. When her body was being taken to the dock, to be shipped back to Brunswick, there was a riot along the route in Kensington. Bricks were thrown and two protesters were shot by Life Guards. Caroline was buried in Brunswick Cathedral and the inscription on her coffin reads: 'The Injured Queen of England'.

A free man once more, George IV continued in his scandalous ways. He exchanged Lady Hertford for Lady Conyngham, who was the same age as Lady Hertford but considerably fatter. Rumours soon circulated that they were deeply in love and he was seen nodding, winking and making eyes at Lady Conyngham in Westminster Abbey while the Archbishop of York was giving a sermon on the sovereign's duty to protect his people from 'the contagion of vice'.

George IV continued to be one of the most unpopular monarchs ever to sit on the throne of England. He had little influence with the Tory and coalition governments during his reign and the prominent Whig Lord Holland said that they encouraged 'every species of satire against him and his mistresses'.

When George IV died in 1830, his obituary in *The Times* said: 'There never was an individual less regretted by his fellow creatures than this deceased king.'

When he was buried, he had left instruction that a picture of Mrs Fitzherbert should be tied on a ribbon around his neck and placed on his heart. Although they had been estranged for many years, Mrs Fitzherbert wept when she heard of the King's instructions.

Jibbing Juries

As law is made in the courtroom
as well as Parliament and other
legislatures, judges like to keep
a firm hand. They are, after all,
the experts – or at least consider
themselves so. But sometimes, juries
will simply not do what they are told.

JAILING THE JURY

Law was made at the Old Bailey in 1670 during the trial of the Quakers William Penn and William Mead, both of whom had been law students. On 14 August they had been doing a spot of preaching in Gracechurch Street after being denied access to their meeting house and were promptly arrested. On 1 September they were called to answer an indictment that said they had 'assembled and congregated . . . a great concourse and tumult of People . . . in contempt of the said Lord the King, and of his Law, to the great disturbance of his Peace, to the great terror and disturbance of many of his Liege people and Subjects, to the ill example of all others, in the like case Offenders, and against the Peace of the said Lord the King, his Crown and Dignity'.

The nine men on the bench included the Lord Mayor of London Sam Starling, a number of his aldermen, the lieutenant of the Tower John Robinson and the recorder John Howel. The proceedings did not start well: when Penn and Mead's tall Quaker hats had been removed, the Mayor ordered one of the officers of the court to put them back on again.

The recorder then asked Penn why he had not taken off his hat. He replied: 'Because I do not believe that to be any respect.'

He was then fined forty marks – £26, thirteen shillings and four pence (over £2,200 today) – for contempt of court.

Penn protested that their hats were off when he came into court.

'If they have been put on since, it was by order from the bench; and therefore not we, but the bench should be fined,' he said.

Mead asked if he had been fined, too. When told he had, he said: 'I desire the jury and all people to take notice of this injustice of the recorder, who spake not to me to pull off my hat, and yet hath he put a fine upon my head.'

The officers who made the arrests were called. They gave evidence of Penn 'speaking to the people' and 'preaching to them'. One said that he had not seen Mead there, so the recorder asked Mead if he was there. He replied by quoting the maxim *'nemo tenetur accusare seipsum'* – 'that no man is bound to accuse himself' – and accused the recorder of trying to ensnare him. The recorder told him to hold his tongue.

Penn then asked the recorder under what law he was being prosecuted. The recorder said the Common Law and insisted he must enter a plea on his indictment, but Penn said the indictment had no foundation in law.

'If it contain the law you say I have broken, why should you decline to produce the law?' he asked.

The record answered that he was 'a saucy fellow'. When Penn continued to argue this point of law, the recorder ordered that he be put in the squalid lock-up next to the courtroom. But Mead continued to press the point.

When the recorder still failed to come up with appropriate statute, Mead turned to the jury and told them what constituted a riot, a rout or an unlawful assembly. It was 'when three, or more, are met together to beat a man, or to enter forcibly into another man's land, to cut down his grass, his wood, or break down his pales'. As no unlawful act was planned, or had taken place, there was no unlawful assembly.

Mead, too, was put in the lock-up. Meanwhile, Penn began shouting that rights under Magna Carta were being denied. Penn and Mead were then consigned to the dungeon, out of earshot.

The recorder then summed up, saying that there was a cast-iron cast and sent the jury out. Eight of them returned after an hour and a half; the other four were dragged back into court. The recorder then picked out Edward Bushel as leader of the dissent faction, while John Robinson told him: 'You deserve to be indicted more than any man that hath been brought to the bar this day.'

The foreman of the jury was then asked for their verdict.

'Guilty of speaking in Gracechurch Street,' he said.

The recorder said this was not good enough, they must reach a verdict on the matter of unlawful assembly, and sent them out again so 'that we may make an end of this troublesome business'.

They returned half an hour later, this time with a written verdict. It said: 'We the Jurors, hereafter named, do find William Penn to be guilty of Speaking or Preaching to an Assembly, met together in Gratious-Street, the 14th of August last 1670, and that William Mead is not guilty of the said Indictment.'

Again, the recorder rejected his verdict and the jury were locked up 'without meat, drink, fire and tobacco'.

'We will have a verdict,' he said, 'or you shall starve for it.'

Penn protested that a jury's verdict should be free, not compelled. If the jury returned with another verdict he would 'affirm that they are perjured men in law'. They returned at seven o'clock the following morning with the same verdict. When the recorder said that this was no verdict, Mead protested: 'How is "not guilty" no verdict?'

The Lord Mayor then threatened to have Bushel's nose cut off. The jury was then ordered to go out again 'and bring in another verdict, or you shall starve; and I will have you carted about the City, as in Edward the third's time'. Being carried around the City in a cart and exposed to the public was a punishment usually reserved for prostitutes.

When the jury returned as seven the following morning, they claimed the foreman said they had already given their verdict in writing. The court then asked again for a verdict. The foreman then gave way – and said they were both not guilty.

The bench then insisted that each of the jurymen answer for themselves. Each of them answered not guilty. The recorder then fined them each forty marks and imprisoned them until they paid.

Penn then demanded to be set free as the jury had found him not guilty, but the recorder said that he was held for his fines.

'Fines for what?'

'For contempt of court.'

Penn then pointed out that, under Magna Carta, no man could be fined unless he had been judged by a jury of his peers. He was locked up again, along with the jury. Penn and Mead's fines were paid by Penn's father Admiral Sir William Penn, the dubious national hero who had taken Jamaica for the Commonwealth. Bushel appealed to Chief Justice Vaughan, who had released the jury, saying: 'A jury must be independent and inscrutably responsible for its verdict free from any threat from the court.'

A plaque in the Old Bailey pays tribute to Bushel's jury. William Penn, of course, took his Quakers to America, where he founded Pennsylvania.

WITHOUT MEAT, DRINK, FIRE . . .

On 13 May 1688 at Lambeth Palace, seven bishops signed a petition defying James II's Declaration of Indulgence, which granted broad religious freedom in England by suspending penal laws enforcing conformity to the Church of England and allowing persons to worship in their homes or chapels as they saw fit. The King had introduced it because he was a Catholic. The Anglican bishops said that the declaration was illegal and demanded it be withdrawn.

When he refused, they had the petition printed and distributed for sale on the streets of London. James charged them with seditious libel and had them locked in the Tower. They were tried before the King's Bench on 29 June. The King himself had checked the jury list, making sure that they were well-to-do men who were likely to be on the side of the Crown.

The Lord Chief Justice allowed the jury some wine before they went out. Then the jury bailiff was sworn in, in accordance with the law. He was told: 'You shall well and truly keep every person sworn in this jury in some private and convenient room without meat, drink, fire, candle or lodging . . .'

The jury were then locked up in the dark, while the solicitor for the defence lurked outside to make sure that the ushers, who were servants of the Crown, did not bribe the jurors with food and drink. At four in the morning, basins of water were sent in so they could wash. They drank the lot.

In the deliberations in the dark, the jurymen had a dilemma. Michael Arnold, a brewer who supplied beer to the palace, said: 'Whatever I do, I am sure to be half ruined. If I say "Not guilty", I shall brew no more for the King; and if I say "Guilty", I shall brew no more for anybody else.'

At first, three members of the jury were in favour of convicting the bishops; nine were in favour of acquitting them. Soon it was just Arnold who wanted to convict. Thomas Austin, a large man, had taken notes during the trial and tried to persuade him to change his mind. Arnold said it was impossible to debate or reason when you were hungry.

'If you come to that,' said Austin as dawn broke, 'look at me. I am the largest and strongest of the twelve; and before I find such a petition as this to be a libel, I will stay here till I am no bigger than a tobacco pipe.'

Arnold eventually gave way. When they returned to court at ten, they found the bishops not guilty, ringing the death knell of the House of Stuart. Six months later, James II fled the country and William of Orange took over. It was not until 1870 that an Act was passed allowing the jury fire and refreshments 'to be procured at their own expense'. And it was not until 1897 that juries were allowed to go home at night – and even then, not in murder cases.

'THIS MUST NOT BE'

On 20 November 1751, the House of Commons sent Alexander Murray to Newgate Prison for misconduct during a by-election. When ordered to kneel to receive sentence, he refused, saying: 'Sir, I beg to be excused; I never kneel but to God.' He was returned to Newgate for two months for contempt, and he was refused release when brought before the House again.

The House then ordered the Attorney-General to try bookseller William Owen for printing and selling a pamphlet called *The Case of the Hon. Alex. Murray, esq; in an Appeal to the People of Great Britain; More Particularly the Inhabitants of the City and Liberty of Westminster*. The House then resolved: 'That the said pamphlet is an impudent, malicious, scandalous, and seditious libel, falsely and most injuriously reflecting up, and aspersing the proceedings of this House, and tending to create misapprehensions of the same in the minds of the people, to the dishonour of this House, and in violation of the privilege thereof.'

The trial took place in the Guildhall under Lord Chief Justice 'Single Joke' Lee – so-called because he was born in 1688 and would say, repeatedly, because he came in with King William, he was bound to be a good Whig, then the ruling party. The Attorney-General argued that to convict Owen of criminal libel it was enough to prove that he had sold the pamphlet, while the defence contended that it was also necessary to prove that the book was libellous.

Lord Chief Justice Lee agreed with the prosecution. Being a good Whig, he ruled that the pamphlet was libellous because Parliament had said it was libellous and instructed the jury to find Owen guilty. The jury went out and came back two hours later with their verdict.

'Gentlemen of the jury, are you agreed on your verdict? Is the defendant guilty or not guilty?' asked the clerk of the court.

'Guilty,' said the foreman.

'You could not do otherwise,' Lord Chief Justice Lee said.

Then the rest of the jury piped up, saying: 'No! No! My Lord! It is all a mistake – we say "Not guilty"!'

'Yes, My Lord, it was a mistake,' said the foreman. 'I meant to say "Not guilty".'

There were cheers from the public gallery.

'My Lord, this must not be,' said the Attorney-General. 'I insist on the jury being called back and asked their opinion on the only question submitted to them.'

'Gentlemen of the jury,' said Lord Chief Justice Lee, 'do you not think the evidence laid before you of Owen's publishing the book by selling it is not sufficient to convince you that the said Owen did sell this book?'

'Not guilty, My Lord,' said the foreman. 'Not guilty.'

'That is our verdict,' chimed the jury, 'and so say we all.'

In the face of such defiance, Lord Chief Justice Lee lost all authority. Not that politicians of either stripe were held in high esteem at the time – both 'Whig' and 'Tory' were turns of abuse. 'Whig' was the Scottish–Gaelic for 'horse thief'; and in the seventeenth century, 'Tory' meant 'a dispossessed Irishman, who became outlaw and subsisted by plundering and killing English settlers and soldiers, a bog-trotter, a rapparee . . .'. William of Orange's successor passed two Acts banning Tories along with robbers and rapparees – Irish irregular soldiers, bandits, robbers or freebooters.

The year after Owen's trial, Alexander Murray of Elibank, fourth son of Alexander Murray, fourth Lord Elibank, was involved in a Jacobite plot to kidnap the King and spent twenty years in exile with Bonnie Prince Charlie.

THE BOUGHT JURYMAN

No sooner had the jury been sworn in at Clerkenwell Green magistrates court on 2 January 1838 when one of the jurors, a Mr H. Wilson, asked to be paid. Addressing Serjeant Adams, the chairman of the bench, he said: 'I should like to know, Mr Chairman, how I am to be indemnified for my loss of time and the trouble and inconvenience I am put to by coming here.'

Adam chose to ignore this interjection and told the clerk to go on with the case.

'It's all very well to say "go on",' said Wilson, 'but I won't go on until I know who is to pay me.'

Patiently, Serjeant Adams explained that jury service was an important public duty and 'one of the most beautiful parts of our admirable constitution for which no remuneration is due'. Then he ordered the case to proceed again.

The defendant, Benjamin Dickinson, was accused of assaulting an officer of the county court. It was an open-and-shut case. Adams summed up quickly and the jury was sent out for what should have been a summary decision, but Wilson refused to give a verdict until he was paid.

Adams then reminded Wilson that, when he was sworn in, he had given an oath that he would return a verdict and that the Bench was perfectly happy to 'place the jury in a locked room without fire or candle until that verdict is delivered'.

Wilson conceded that he had sworn an oath to

241

deliver a verdict, but he did not say when he would deliver it – and he would do so when he was well and truly ready.

Serjeant Adams then ordered the jury to be removed and locked in a room until they had come to a decision. The rest of the jury appealed to Adams, then begged Wilson not to be so unreasonable. They then said that they would have a whip round and pay Wilson themselves, so they could go home. Adams forbade this. Wilson then refused to leave the jury box.

As court officers closed in to remove him bodily, he rose and went out. They were locked in the jury room, where further deliberations were private. Fifteen minutes later, they returned a guilty verdict and Wilson went away with a smile on his face. There were suspicions that money had changed hands behind closed doors, but Serjeant Adams did not enquire into the matter.

"HIS FIRST OFFENCE."

MR. DEVINE SPEAKING FOR THE
PRISONER.

Cautionary Cases

All human folly has been paraded
through the law courts of London.
Sometimes it is difficult to know where
the serious business of administering
justice ends and where farce begins.

THE HAMMERSMITH GHOST

When law is made in the courts by precedent it some-times takes the statute a long time to catch up. One such instance began after a number of people claimed to have seen – and even been attacked – by a ghost in Hammersmith in 1803. It was thought to be the spectre of a suicide victim, who had mistakenly been buried on consecrated ground, where self-killers are not supposed to rest easy. A coachman said he saw a horrible creature with horns and glassy eyes, and fled leaving his eight horses and six passengers in the greatest danger. After that, no one moved around Hammersmith at night unarmed.

On 3 January 1804, the watchman William Girdler and his friend, exciseman Francis Smith, were out on patrol in Black Lion Lane when they saw a mysterious figure that was white from head to foot. After a shouted warning, Smith fired. He had shot and killed Thomas Millwood, a twenty-three-year-old plasterer returning from work, whose hands, face and clothes were covered with the materials of his trade. Discovering his mistake, Smith surrendered to a passing wine merchant and they repaired to the Black Lion public house to await the law.

Ten days later, Smith appeared in the Old Bailey, charged with murder. Witnesses testified as to the terri-fying aspect of the ghost, while others were called to confirm the good character of Francis Smith.

Nevertheless, Lord Chief Baron instructed the jury that, if Smith had fired intentionally, they were to return a verdict of guilty.

The jury returned after an hour with the verdict of manslaughter. The bench would not accept this. Under the law the verdict must be 'guilty of murder' or 'a total acquittal from want of evidence'. The jury went out again and returned with a guilty verdict. The sentence of death was pronounced, and Smith's body was to be given to the surgeons for dissection. However, the following day the King commuted the sentence to one year's hard labour.

The ghost himself then came forward. He was an elderly shoemaker named John Graham who had taken to wearing a white sheet to scare his apprentice who, in turn, had been scaring the Graham children.

For 180 years, the verdict was discussed in legal circles and was the subject of countless learned articles. However, the matter was resolved in 1984, when an appeal court overturned the conviction of Gladstone Williams for actual bodily harm when he intervened on behalf of a young man being dragged along the street by another man, who was, in fact, attempting to apprehend a suspected thief.

The decision was confirmed by the Privy Council, sitting in London, in the case of Beckford v The Queen. The case concerned a policeman in Jamaica who had shot and killed a man whom he believed had a gun. The judge had directed that the jury must decide whether that belief was 'reasonably held'. The Privy Council said that it was only necessary that the defendant 'honestly believed' the man had a gun. This was then incorporated into law in the 2008 Criminal Justice and Immigration Act.

MY SON-IN-LAW THE DEFENDANT

In the Old Bailey in December 1812, the twenty-four-year-old Marquess of Sligo was tried for enticing British sailors from their duty during time of war. Two years earlier, at the height of the Napoleonic Wars, he had persuaded two sailors at Gibraltar to desert their warship and join him on his yacht. The trial was presided over by Lord Chief Justice Ellenborough, who sat with Sir William Scott, the leading maritime jurist of the day.

The Dowager Marchioness of Sligo turned up in court, aiming to soften the heart of the bench with her pleas. It worked – up to a point. Although Lord Sligo was fined £5,000 and sentenced to four months in Newgate, when he was released he found Sir William had married his mother.

Sligo went on to become governor of Jamaica when the slaves were freed and Sligoville, there, is named after him.

THE CONCENTRATED MIND

While a devout Christian and editor of the *Christian* magazine, the Reverend Doctor William Dodd was not good when it came to money. The chaplain to the King, he was struck off when he offered three thousand guineas to the Lord Chancellor for the living of St George's, Hanover Square. Instead he set up the Charlotte Chapel in the Italianate suburb of Pimlico, becoming known as the 'macaroni clergyman' and a figure of public ridicule.

Short of money, he borrowed against a bond in the name of his former pupil, the Earl of Chesterfield. However, the banker spotted a small blot and had the document rewritten. When it was presented to the Earl for signature, he denied all knowledge of it. Dodd immediately confessed and was told that he would be saved from the gallows if he paid back the money.

He did this, but in the meantime was imprisoned in the Wood Street Compter, a debtor's prison in the City. Although no witnesses were called to testify against him, he was convicted of forgery. Despite the assistance of Dr Johnson, he was sentenced to death, though he was allowed the privilege of travelling to Tyburn in his own carriage with the hearse carrying his coffin preceding him.

Johnson also ghostwrote *The Convict's Address to his Unhappy Brethren* for Dodd. When accused of this subterfuge, Johnson covered his tracks with the famous remark: 'Depend upon it, Sir, when a man knows he is to be hanged in a fortnight, it concentrates his mind wonderfully.'

NO NOTES

The Gordon Riots of 1780 did more damage to London than anything between the Great Fire of London in 1666 and the Blitz of 1940–41. The anti-Catholic riots lasted a week, causing great damage to property and leaving some five hundred casualties. Lord George Gordon, head of the Protestant Association formed in opposition to the Catholic Relief Act of 1778, was tried for high treason for instigating the violence.

The star witness for the Crown was the printer William Hay, who testified that, at meetings, Gordon had said: 'The King has broken his coronation oath' – where the monarch promises to 'maintain and preserve inviolable the settlement of the Church of England'; 'By assenting himself to the Act for tolerating Catholics, the King has brought himself to the same pass as James II' – who was forced from office because he was a Catholic; and 'Stick steadily to your good and glorious cause'.

Cross-questioned by counsel for the defence, Lloyd Kenyon, Hay said that he had been at a meeting of the Protestant Association on 21 January 1780, where Gordon had been present.

Kenyon: Reflect carefully. Did you see him there or not?

Hay: I think I saw him there.

Kenyon: Be on your guard. Did you see him there or not?

Hay: I could speak with more certainty if I might look at my notes.

Kenyon: Notes? Notes? How came you to take notes?

Hay: I will tell you very freely. Originally, my curiosity led me to those meetings, but in time I came to dread and foresee the consequences of them.

Kenyon: When did you first foresee the consequences?

Hay: At a meeting on the twentieth of February.

Kenyon: If that was the first time you were moved to take notes, how would your notes help you with the twenty-first of January?

Hay: I took notes at all the meetings right from the tenth of December.

Kenyon: Why did you take notes before you foresaw the consequences?

Hay: Whenever I go to public meetings, I take notes.

Kenyon: Give me an instance, other than these. Tell me where and when you have taken notes before.

(There was no answer.)

Kenyon: Tell me where and when.

(Again, there was no answer.)

Kenyon: Tell me where and when.

Hay: At the General Assembly of the Church of Scotland. When I was much younger – twenty-two years ago.

The jury found this hard to believe. Plainly, Hay was a spy and they acquitted Lord Gordon. But he continued to fall foul of the law. In 1786, Gordon was excommunicated from the Church of England for refusing to bear witness in an ecclesiastical suit and converted to Judaism.

The following year, he was convicted of libelling the Queen of France, the French Ambassador in London and the Administration of Justice in England. He jumped bail, but returned to London to suffer five years in Newgate. In prison he lived comfortably, giving dinners and dances. Refusing help from his family, he brought two Jews to provide securities for his good behaviour at the end of his sentence. The court would not accept them. Returned to Newgate, he died there of typhoid fever in 1793.

THE DERBY'S DAY IN COURT

Every Londoner's favourite race is the Derby, which is held annually outside the city on Epsom Downs. But the race of 1844 was won, not on the Downs, but in a courtroom in Westminster. The favourite, Ratan, was mysteriously poisoned in his stable before the race. Another contender, Leander, was kicked by Running Rein, who went on to win, and had to be destroyed, but was subsequently discovered to have been a four-year-old – thus ineligible as the race is for three-year-old colts and fillies.

Colonel Jonathan Peel, the owner of Orlando, who came second, then protested that the winner was another four-year-old substituted for Running Rein. The Jockey Club froze the prize money and the case was tried in the Court of Chancery at Westminster under the Baron of the Exchequer, Sir Edward Hall Alderson, an experienced judge of horse flesh.

When the results of inspection were disputed, Alderson called for Running Rein to appear in court. The trainer then said that the horse had been taken away on the verbal order of the owner before the court order arrived. Two days later, the owner said that the horse was still missing, presumed stolen.

Baron Alderson found in favour of Colonel Peel, awarding him the prize money. So Orlando became the winner of the Derby of 1844.

PITY ON FOREIGNERS

While duelling had fallen out of fashion in the nineteenth century, it was not outlawed. However, in 1852, Emmanuel Barthélemy, who fled to London from Paris after killing a policeman to escape deportation to Devil's Island, fell out with fellow émigré, Frederic Cournet. They took a train out to Windsor, where they fought a duel on Englefield Green and Cournet was killed. This was all very well out in the depths of Berkshire, but when Barthélemy and the seconds arrived back at Waterloo Station, carrying the blooded rapiers, they were arrested.

Russian exile Alexander Herzen attended an English court for the first time to see the Lord Chief Justice in action. 'Old Lord Campbell, who had grown grey and wrinkled in his judicial armchair, reading in an impassive voice with a Scotch accent the most frightening evidences, and unravelling the most complex cases with palpable clarity – he was to be out-witted by a handful of Parisian clubistes!' Herzen wrote. 'Lord Campbell, who never raises his voice, never loses his temper, never smiles, and only permits himself at the most absurd or critical moments to blow his nose ... Lord Campbell with the face of a peevish old woman, in which if you look intently you can clearly discern the celebrated metamorphosis that so unpleasantly surprised Little Red Riding Hood; you see that it is not grandmamma at all, but a wolf in a wig, a woman's dressing-gown and a fur-trimmed jacket.'

Barthélemy and the seconds at the duel were duly convicted of manslaughter, but Lord Campbell, pitying the ignorant foreigners, sentenced them to just two months in prison. Two years later, in Warren Street, Barthélemy shot and killed a tradesman and the policeman who tried to arrest him. He was publicly hanged at Newgate on 22 January 1855.

MAIDEN TRIBUTE

In 1885, W. T. Stead, the crusading editor of the *Pall Mall Gazette*, sought to expose child prostitution in London with a series of articles called 'The Maiden Tribute of Modern Babylon'. To demonstrate how easy it was to procure a child from those purposes, he arranged to purchase thirteen-year-old Eliza Armstrong, the daughter of a chimney sweep, for just £5. The girl was then given to the care of the Salvation Army and taken to France on holiday.

Soon afterwards, *Lloyd's News* carried the story of Eliza's mother, who was searching for the girl. Stead was accused of kidnapping. He and his companions – including William Booth, founder of the Salvation Army – were prosecuted. After a long and detailed trial, Stead was sentenced to three months' imprisonment. On his release, he continued his career in campaigning journalism. He died on board the *Titanic* and was last seen reading quietly in the first-class smoking room as the ship went down.

COSTLY CUSSING

In 1722, James Sparling of the parish of St James, Clerkenwell, was convicted of uttering fifty-four oaths and 160 curses within ten days and fined £21 eight shillings – nearly £2,000 today. However, a motion was made to quash the conviction on the grounds that he had been fined two shillings an oath, whereas the statute said that the penalty was just one shilling an oath where the offender was 'a servant, labourer, common soldier, or seaman'. Sparling was a leather-dresser, but the defence argued that he was of that social class and such a fine would destroy him.

Tiring of the matter, the court threw out the conviction on the grounds that the oaths and curses had not been written down, so the judge could not assess whether they were seditious or blasphemous.

Departed Rib

Before divorce was available to those other than the super-rich, it was not uncommon for husbands to sell their wives, even in the centre of London. *The Times* of 18 July 1797 reported that a butcher had 'exposed his wife to sale in Smithfield Market, near the Ram Inn, with a halter about her neck, and one about her waist which tied her to the railing . . . a hog driver was the happy purchaser, who gave the husband three guineas and a crown for his departed rib'. These sales were against the law, but they were often pre-arranged and the buyer was the wife's lover. Lord Mansfield, the Lord Chief Justice, considered such an arrangement a criminal conspiracy.

Over-long Submission

At a case at Westminster Hall in 1596, the barrister used 120 sheets of paper for submission, which the court felt could have been dealt with in sixteen sheets. So it was ordered that the Lord Keeper 'shall bring him unto Westminster Hall . . . and there and then shall cut a hole in the middle of the same engrossed replication ... and put the said Richard's head through the same hole ... and shall show him at the bar of every of the three courts within the Hall'.

JENNENS V JENNENS

When William Jennens died in 1798 he was thought to be the richest commoner in England, worth some £2 million – over £200 million now. A will was found in his coat pocket, but it was not signed, apparently because when he went to his solicitor to have it witnessed, he had forgotten to take his glasses. So the subsequent dispute by members of the family passed to the Court of Chancery, where litigation dragged on for over a century until the entire fortune was swallowed up by lawyers' fees. This case was the inspiration for the fictional case of Jarndyce v Jarndyce in Charles Dickens' *Bleak House*, published in 1852–53.

FOR FASHION'S SAKE

Lord Mansfield was not considered a lenient judge, but he was shocked at the thought of killing a man for a trifling theft. Trying a prisoner at the Old Bailey on the charge of stealing in a dwelling-house a gold trinket to the value of forty shillings (£2) – when this was a capital offence – he advised the jury to find it to be worth less. The prosecutor exclaimed with indignation, 'Under forty shillings, My Lord! Why, the fashion alone cost me more than double the sum.'

'God forbid, gentlemen, we should hang a man for fashion's sake,' Lord Mansfield observed to the jury.

ABOVE THE LAW

In his *Lives of the Most Eminent English Poets*, Samuel Johnson related in his entry on Charles Sackville, Lord Dorset:

> Sackville, who was then Lord Buckhurst, with Sir Charles Sedley and Sir Thomas Ogle, got drunk at the Cock, in Bow Street, by Covent Garden, and going into the balcony exposed themselves to the populace in very indecent postures. At last, as they grew warmer, Sedley stood forth naked, and harangued the populace in such profane language, that the publick indignation was awakened; the crowd attempted to force the door, and being repulsed, drove in the performers with stones, and broke the windows of the house. For this misdemeanour they were indicted, and Sedley was fined five hundred pounds; what was the sentence of the others is not known.

According to Samuel Pepys, Sedley

showed his nakedness – acting all the postures of lust and buggery that could be imagined, and abusing of scripture and, as it were, from thence preaching a Mountebanke sermon from that pulpitt, saying that there he hath to sell such a powder as should make all the cunts in town run after him, a thousand people standing underneath to see and hear him. And that being done, he took a glass of wine and washed his prick in it and then drank it off, and then took another and drank the King's health.

Sedley went on to become Speaker of the House of Commons.

IS EATING PEOPLE ILLEGAL?

This was the matter the High Court sitting in the Royal Courts of Justice in the Strand had to decide in 1884. The incident it was concerned with had happened five months earlier, thousands of miles away in the South Atlantic.

On 5 July 1884, the 52-foot yacht *Mignonette* had sunk in a gale nearly two thousand miles from land. The captain Thomas Dudley had taken to an open boat with Edwin Stephens, Ned Brooks and cabin boy Richard Parker, who was seventeen.

After eleven days adrift, their food had run out. Two days later, they had run out of fresh water. Five days after that, they began to discuss which one of their number they should sacrifice and eat. Otherwise all four were certain to perish. Dudley and Stephens decided to draw straws. Brooks would have nothing to do with it and Parker was too weak to take part in the discussion.

By day twenty, Dudley and Stephens decided that they could hold out no longer. By this time Parker was close to death and he had no family dependent on him. They cut his throat. Although Brooks had no part in the slaughter, he joined in the feast and drank the cabin boy's blood along with the other two. Four days later, they were rescued by the German barque *Montezuma*, which took them to Falmouth, where they were greeted as returning heroes. While it was clear that Dudley and Stephens should be charged with murder, there was a clamour for their acquittal. They had, after all, killed the boy out of necessity. It was better that one of them die, rather than all four.

The original trial took place at the Exeter Assizes on 6 November, where the judge Baron Huddleston took the unusual step of asking the jury to return a 'special verdict'. They were to decide merely on the facts of the case. The matter of defendants' guilt or innocence was to be reserved for the High Court.

In the Queen's Bench Division of the High Court of Justice in London, five judges were to decide whether the doctrine of necessity overrode the normal prohibition on murder. Leading the panel was the Lord Chief Justice, Lord Coleridge.

'It is admitted that the deliberate killing of this unoffending and unresisting boy was clearly murder, unless the killing can be justified by some well-recognised excuse admitted by the law,' he said. 'It is further admitted that there was in this case no such excuse, unless the killing was justified by what has been called "necessity".'

But that left a question.

'Who is to be the judge of this sort of necessity? By what measure is the comparative value of lives to be measured? Is it to be strength, or intellect or what? It is plain that the principle leaves to him who is to profit by it to determine the necessity which will justify him in deliberately taking another's life to save his own. In this case the weakest, the youngest, the most unresisting, was chosen. Was it more necessary to kill him than one of the grown men? The answer must be "No".'

The panel decided that Dudley and Stephens had committed wilful murder and that there was no legal justification for what they had done. Lord Coleridge then had no alternative but to pass a sentence of death on them. However, he recommended clemency to the Crown and they served just six months without hard labour.

A MAN OF CHARACTER

In the *Curiosities of Law and Lawyers*, published in Fetter Lane, off Fleet Street in 1896, the author Croake James records an anecdote he heads: 'Hanged Though He Had £200'. It says:

Mr. Selwin, who had stood for the office of Chamberlain of London but lost the election, told this story. 'I was once requested by a man under sentence of death in Newgate to come and see him in his cell, and, in pure humanity, I made him a visit. The man briefly informed me that he had been convicted of felony, and daily expected the warrant of his execution. "But," he said, 'I have £200, and you are a man of character, and had the court interest when you stood for chamberlain. I should therefore hope it is in your power to get me off." I was struck with so strange a notion, and to enable myself to account for it, asked if there were any alleviating circumstances in the case. The man peevishly answered, no, but he had inquired into the history of the place where he was, and could not find any that any one who had £200 was ever hanged. I told him it was out of my power to help him, and bade him farewell. Yet he found means after all to escape punishment.'

VOTES FOR WOMEN

The rights of women had a small advance in 1737 when Sarah Bly stood against John Olive to be sexton of the parish of St Botolph in the City of London. The question was, not only could she serve as sexton, but whether women were allowed to vote. This was because, while John Olive had 174 male votes and 22 female, Sarah Bly had 169 male votes and 40 female.

Adjudicating, Chief Justice Lee said:

> I am clearly of the opinion that a woman may be sexton of a parish. Women have held much higher offices, and, indeed, almost all offices of the kingdom, as Queen, Marshal, Great Chamberlain, Great Constable, Champion of England, Commissioner of Sewers, keeper of a prison, and returning officer for Members of Parliament. Moreover it would be strange if a woman may fill the officer and yet should be disqualified to vote for it. The election of Members of Parliament and coroners stands on special grounds. No woman has ever sat in parliament or voted for Members of Parliament, and we must presume that when the franchise was first created, it was confined to the male sex. But no such reason exists as to the office of sexton.

RUINED BY ACQUITTAL

In the 1879, the new rising star of the Liberal Party was Sir Charles Wentworth Dilke. Benjamin Disraeli saw him as a future prime minister. But he was brought down by a court case, even though the allegations against him were never proved.

In July 1885, Dilke was the youngest Cabinet minister and privy councillor, and tipped as William Ewart Gladstone's heir apparent. Then he was named in a divorce case of twenty-two-year-old Virginia Crawford, sister of his brother's widow.

Virginia was the daughter of a Tyneside ship owner, who had been forced to marry Donald Crawford, a Liberal MP twice her age. But this did not inhibit her. For years, she and her sister Helen amused themselves with medical students from a nearby hospital. They also visited a brothel in Knightsbridge, where they were both entertained by one Captain Henry Forster.

Dilke and Virginia may well have been lovers. He visited her while her husband was away and he was certainly the lover of her mother, Mrs Eustace Smith. Things were seldom as strait-laced in the Victorian era as one imagines. But when Virginia's husband filed for divorce, Dilke feared that his political career was over.

'In the case of a public man, a charge is always believed by many, even though disproved, and I should be weighted by it throughout life,' he wrote.

However, he was determined to fight. He was engaged to be married at the time to Mrs Emilia Patterson, the widow of the rector of Lincoln College, who he had been wooing for ten years. This was scandalous enough as, for most of that time, her husband had been alive.

Virginia's husband Donald Crawford knew nothing of his wife's affair with Captain Forster or her other dalliances. But he had received a series of anonymous letters telling him to 'beware of the member from Chelsea – Dilke'.

Dilke and his fiancée Emilia had also being receiving anonymous letters which sought to disrupt their marriage plans. A staunch republican, Dilke had spoken out against the royal family and suspected his harassment was an establishment plot, though there were other suspects.

'In my belief the conspiracy comes from a woman who wanted me to marry her,' Dilke wrote to his fiancée. The suspect was a Mrs Rogerson, a friend of Virginia Crawford's, who may well have been another of Dilke's lovers.

When Crawford received a fourth letter naming Forster as his wife's lover, he confronted her. She denied that Forster was her lover but, seemingly eager for divorce, admitted to adultery with Dilke. She alleged that Dilke had also had a string of other lovers, including her mother – which was true – and one of his maids called Sarah Gray. Dilke was plainly a busy man, and not just in Whitehall.

Even though Dilke was being cited in a divorce case, Emilia went ahead and married him in Oxford in October 1885. The following month, after writing to his constituents denying the charges of adultery, Dilke was re-elected MP for Chelsea. However, as he had not yet cleared his name, Gladstone, a stickler for propriety – in others, at least – dropped him from his government.

When the case opened in February 1886, Virginia Crawford was not present. However, Crawford said that he had wrung a confession from her. He told the court that his wife admitted going to an 'assignation house' off Tottenham Court Road with Dilke. She had also visited him at his house in Sloane Street and entertained him in their own home when he had been away, though she was sketchy on the detail.

What turned the trial from an ordinary divorce case into a huge Victorian scandal was one new and sensational allegation. Crawford said that Dilke had forced his wife into a threesome with a serving girl called Fanny Stock and had taught her 'every French vice'. Asked who Fanny was, his wife had said that she was Dilke's mistress. Virginia had also said that Dilke had compared Fanny to her mother.

All this was hearsay evidence. It was simply Crawford repeating what he alleged his wife had said. He had no evidence – not even a love letter or a note arranging an assignation in Dilke's hand. The only witness he could produce was his wife's parlour maid, Ann Jameson. She said that when Mr Crawford was out of town, Mrs Crawford stayed out at night. Dilke had also visited her at her house. Under cross-examination, however, it transpired that these were normal social visits. Captain Forster also visited, and Ann had handled correspondence between Mrs Crawford and Captain Forster. There was none with Dilke.

As the redoubtable Fanny had disappeared, the only witness the defence could call was Dilke himself. But he did not want to take the stand and risk being asked questions concerning his relationship with Mrs Eustace Smith.

Explaining his client's reluctance to take the stand, Dilke's barrister, the Attorney General Sir Charles Russell, said: 'In the life of any man there may be found to have been possible indiscretions.'

He moved to have Dilke's name stricken from the divorce petition. The judge agreed to do so. He granted a decree nisi, finding that, while Mrs Crawford had committed adultery, there was no admissible evidence to indicate that she had done so with Dilke. And he ordered that his costs be paid for by Mr Crawford as he had accused Dilke of adultery without reasonable grounds for suspicion.

So, legally, Dilke was not guilty of adultery, but Russell's decision not to put his client on the stand was a fatal error of judgement. Although Dilke had repeatedly denied sleeping with Mrs Crawford, verbally and in writing, that was not the same as saying it in the witness box while under oath.

The press seized upon Russell's remark – that 'In the life of any man there may be found to have been possible indiscretions' – but omitted the word 'possible'. In Victorian England, this was tantamount to admitting that he had committed adultery with someone, even if it was not the errant wife in the Crawford case. And the case stayed in the news because it was found that Mrs Crawford had been guilty of adultery with someone and the papers wanted to know with whom.

The *Manchester Guardian* condemned Dilke's behaviour at the trial and said: 'To ask us on the strength of this evasion to welcome him back as a leader of the Liberal Party is too strong a draft on our credulity and good nature.'

A Liberal Association in Scotland passed a resolution condemning any move to have Dilke back in a Liberal cabinet, saying it would condone things that were 'unrighteous and wrong'. But it was the campaigning editor of the *Pall Mall Gazette* and fiery moralist W. T. Stead who pulled out all the stops. He wrote: 'Grave imputations were stated publicly in open court, but there was no detailed reply. Far from having been disproved, they have not even been denied in the witness box.'

He was backed in his moral outrage by General Booth, founder of the Salvation Army, who condemned the Dilke scandal as 'a shameful combination of lust, fraud and falsehood'. With Booth's blessing, Stead called for the member for Chelsea's resignation.

'We are willing to believe that the more terrible part of the charge brought against him is exaggerated,' Stead wrote, charitably. 'But if that charge in its entirety were true, we should not exaggerate the universal sentiment that the man against whom so frightful an accusation could lie is a worse criminal than most of the murderers who swing in Newgate.'

Dilke considered a libel suit, but was afraid that a courtroom would simply give Stead another soapbox. Stead was a man who enjoyed martyrdom. After all, he had recently been to jail for three months for buying a thirteen-year-old girl for £5 from her parents to expose child prostitution.

In an effort to clear his name, Dilke went to the Queen's proctor, who had the power to annul a decree nisi before the decree absolute was granted. Dilke persuaded him to intervene on the grounds that the divorce had been granted on the grounds of adultery, over an act that the judge had admitted in court had not taken place.

The proctor ordered a second hearing and Dilke was optimistic. Fanny Stock had been found and she was willing to deny the three-in-a-bed romp. He also had powerful new evidence about Mrs Crawford's affair with Captain Forster, which she still sought to deny.

But Dilke and his lawyers had made another mistake. As the judge in the original case had stricken Dilke's name from the petition, he was no longer party to the action. His lawyers could not cross-examine Mrs Crawford, nor could they call any witnesses.

In the General Election of 9 July 1886, Dilke lost his seat. Seven days later, the trial started. Dilke then found himself at another unforeseen disadvantage. As he was trying to overturn a decree nisi granted on the grounds of adultery, the prosecutor had to try and prove that there had been no adultery, while Mrs Crawford, who now wanted a divorce, made the case that there had.

Dilke was the first witness to be called to the stand. In front of a packed courtroom, he denied sleeping with Mrs Crawford. He also denied sleeping with Fanny Stock and Sarah Gray. But when asked whether he had slept with Virginia Crawford's mother, Mrs Eustice Smith, he refused to answer. The judge ordered him to. Eventually, he had to admit to the affair.

Then Mrs Crawford was called to the stand. This time she had her story together. The assignation house where she had gone with Dilke was in Warren Street, off Tottenham Court Road, she said. She even sketched a plan of the bedroom there. She also remembered the dates and places of other assignations. And she stuck to her story that she had taken part in a threesome at Dilke's Sloane Street home with Fanny Stock.

This time, she also admitted adultery with Captain Forster, but denied that she had invented the story about having slept with Dilke to protect him. Forster was called and confirmed the affair, but denied that they hoped to marry. He was engaged to a Miss Smith Barry at the time. Mrs Crawford called three other witnesses, who said that they had seen Dilke go into the assignation house at 65 Warren Street on other occasions with other women. Dilke had no opportunity to refute these fresh allegations and his lawyer could not probe them as he had no right to cross-examination. Dilke's reputation was now irreparably damaged.

The trial lasted a week. It reached its climax in a summing-up from Mrs Crawford's barrister, Henry Matthews QC. By Mrs Crawford's confession, he said, Dilke 'was charged not merely with adultery, but with having committed adultery with the child of one friend and the wife of another ... he was charged with having done with an English lady what any man of proper feeling would shrink from doing with a prostitute in a French brothel, and yet he was silent.'

At this point Russell leapt to his feet to object, but the judge ordered him to sit down. Dilke was not a party to the case and had no right to legal representation.

'The burden of proof was on the Queen's Proctor who, in order to be successful, must show conclusively that Mrs Crawford had not committed adultery with Sir Charles Dilke,' Matthews continued. 'The jury could only give a verdict against my client if they believed that Mrs Crawford was a perjured witness and that a conspiracy existed to blast the life of a pure and innocent man.'

By this time, Dilke's character had been so irredeemably blackened that no one believed him to be a 'pure and innocent man'.

The prosecution was left with an impossible task. How could it prove that Dilke had not committed adultery with Mrs Crawford? Mrs Crawford had already admitted adultery with Captain Forster, who had admitted it, too. So Mr Crawford could have his divorce. What did it matter if Mrs Crawford had committed adultery with two people, or only one?

For that matter, Dilke had admitted adultery with Mrs Eustice Smith, why not with Mrs Crawford? What did it matter, if he had partaken in extramarital sex with two people, or only one?

The judge hammered the last nail into Dilke's political coffin. He drew the jury's attention to Dilke's reluctance to take the stand in the first trial and asked: 'If you were to hear such a statement made involving your honour ... would you accept the advice of your counsel to say nothing? Would you allow the court to be deceived and a tissue of falsehoods to be put forward as the truth?'

Upstanding Victorian gentleman to a man, the jury took just fifteen minutes to answer no. They found that the decree nisi was not pronounced contrary to the justice of the case. Dilke had failed to get it overturned. Although no real evidence had ever been put that he had committed adultery, it was generally assumed that he had and was deemed to be lying.

Dilke did manage to get himself re-elected to Parliament for the Forest of Dean in 1892. He remained in Parliament until his death in 1911, but never again held office. Virginia Crawford began a political career of her own. She became a writer and a Labour councillor, and was such a vociferous campaigner against Fascism that she was blacklisted by Mussolini. She died in 1948.

Rational Bloomers

In 1899, a case came before Surrey Assizes concerning Lady Harberton, who had been barred from a pub for wearing 'ration bloomers' – known at the time as 'rationals'. These were very baggy trousers clinched at or below the knee. They had been championed by American social reformer Amelia Jenks Bloomer, who gave her name – or rather her husband's name – to the garment.

Lady Harberton was the treasurer of the Rational Dress Society. She donned a pair of bloomers for a cycling trip through the Home Countries on the grounds that this costume was more practical for bicycling than the voluminous skirts that were in fashion at the time.

On 27 October 1898, she stopped at the Hautboy Hotel in Ockham for lunch, but the proprieter, Martha Sprague, refused her entry to the main 'coffee room' on the grounds of indecency. In a test case, Mrs Sprague was prosecuted for refusing a guest entry to her inn without good reason.

Lord Coleridge QC, leading the prosecution, showed the jury a photograph of Lady Harberton in her bloomers, demonstrating that, far from being indecent, she was clothed 'from the crown of her head to the soles of her feet'. Looking to the future, he argued that one day all womanhood would adopt and admire rational dress and, if they found Lady Harberton's bloomers indecent, the jury risked being judged 'purblind and perverted' by future generations.

However, the court then heard that Lady Harberton had been offered a table in the parlour at the back of the pub to take lunch, but had refused it because the parlour smelled 'abominable' and there were four men in it – one of whom might have been 'a working man'. So the jury acquitted Mrs Sprague on the grounds that she had not turned away a customer for wearing bloomers, she had merely offered her a table in a room she did not like.

DISHONOUR AMONG THIEVES

There was crime in the outer suburbs and some sought redress in the city. In 1725, there was a falling out between two highwaymen, who took the matter to law.

The plaintiff, a man named John Everet, consulted attorney William Wreathock who, in turn, instructed counsel Jonathan Collins to draw up a bill for the Court of Exchequer, a court set up in Westminster by William the Conqueror.

In a statement of facts 'your orator' – Everet claimed that he was 'skilled in dealing in several sorts of commodities' – particularly rings, watches, precious metals and the like. He also claimed that the defendant, Joseph Williams, 'knowing your orator's great care, diligence and industry in managing the said dealings', had asked to become his partner and they entered into an oral agreement to go into business together. They agreed that they should provide 'all sort of necessaries at the joined and equal expense of both such as horses, bridles, saddles, assistants and servants'. Equally, all their expenses on the road and in taverns, inns, alehouses, markets and fairs would be divided equally between them.

The bill further alleged 'that pursuant to the said agreement your orator and the said Joseph Williams went on and proceeded jointly in the said dealings with good success on Hounslow Heath, where they dealt with a gentleman for a gold watch'. Then they proceeded to Finchley, which Williams had told the plaintiff 'was a good and convenient place to deal in, and that commodities were very plenty'. Their dealings there were 'almost all gain to them' and they 'dealt with several gentlemen for divers watches, rings, swords, canes, hats, cloaks, horses, bridles, saddles and other things to the value of £200 and upwards'.

After about a month, they moved on to Blackheath, where Williams had heard that there was a gentleman who had a good horse, saddle, bridle, watch, sword, cane and other things to dispose of which 'might be had for little or no money, in case they could prevail on the said gentleman to part with the said things'. Everet said that, indeed, 'after some small discourse with the said gentleman' he agreed to part with them 'at a very cheap rate'.

Everet and Williams continued about their business in Bagshot, Salisbury, Hampstead and other places, accumulating over £2,000. But when they parted at Michaelmas, Everet maintained that Williams 'began to shuffle with him' and 'would not come to a fair account touching and concerning the said partnership'. The matter, Everet said, was 'relievable only in the Court of Equity before Your Honours where just discoveries are made, frauds detected and just accounts settled.'

Everet's lawyers expected the threat of suit alone would force Williams to settle out of court. But he held his nerve. His attorney persuaded the court to refer the matter to the King's Remembrancer, the chief official of the court whose post was created in 1154, as the bill was 'a scandal and an impertinence'. The action was dismissed and the plaintiff's attorneys were fined £50 each, while his counsel, Collins, was ordered to pay costs, though he had kept away from the hearings. This is believed to be the only case where the barrister has had to pay up.

Williams continued in his chosen trade and was hanged at Maidstone two years later. Everet was hanged at Tyburn for a highway robbery in Hampstead in 1730. Five years later his attorney, William Wreathock, was also condemned to death for highway robbery. The sentence was commuted to transportation for life. He returned with a royal pardon and practised again as a solicitor, although he was eventually struck off.

The Court of the Exchequer closed in 1873 and its jurisdiction was transferred to the Exchequer Division of the High Court of Justice. The post of Queen's Remembrancer is held by the Senior Master of the Queen's Bench Division of the High Court.

NO WORD OF A LIE

Another highwayman was equally foolhardy. In 1704, he took an action for slander against a man who had accused him of being a highwayman. Once the evidence had been heard in court, the judge decided that the plaintiff was indeed a highwayman. He was arrested and taken to Newgate. At the next sessions, he was convicted and hanged.

NON-PAYMENT OF BRIBE

The courts are more lenient with their own. In 1760, a sheriff's bailiff sued in a Stepney Court for the recovery of a bribe he had been promised for granting bail. The court found in his favour awarding his £14 19s – 'as the jurisdiction of the court did not extend to £5'. However, the King's Bench overturned the ruling 'with much indignation', maintaining that the court should have punished the bribe-taking bailiff.

A Special Appeal

In 1722, highwayman John Hartley was convicted of stealing the clothes of a journeyman tailor and leaving him tied naked to a tree in Harrow. He and an accomplice were caught trying to sell them in a pub in Fore Street, Edmonton. Although there was no doubt of his guilt, a special appeal was made on his behalf. Six attractive young women, dressed in white, went to St James's Palace to present a petition for clemency. Their appearance alone guaranteed their admittance. They told the King that, if he pardoned the highwayman, they would draw lots to see who would be Hartley's wife. But George I was not moved. He told them that the prisoner was more deserving of the gallows than a wife and he was hanged at Tyburn on 4 May.

Air Too Pure?

In 1772, a slave named James Somerset was 'confined in irons on board a ship called *Ann and Mary*, John Knowles commander, lying in the Thames, and bound for Jamaica'. In court it was argued that a courtier in the reign of Elizabeth I had successfully contended that the air of England was 'too pure for a slave to breathe in'. Consequently, Lord Mansfield ordered him to be set free.

Sitting with Mansfield was Serjeant-at-law William Davy, who argued that if a slave was brought to England from Africa or America by their master, they would automatically be freed. But if they escaped and came to England, they would not.

Slaves were freed through the British Empire by the Slavery Abolition Act of 1833 and slave owners were compensated by £20 million from public funds; slaves were not.

A Barony Bounces Back

The Duke of Wharton had joined James Edward Stuart, the Old Pretender, in exile, so he did not appear in court in Middlesex to answer an indictment for treason in 1729 and was outlawed. Two years later, he died without issue, so his titles of duke, earl and marquis died with him. But he also had a barony which, were it not for the fact that he was outlawed, could be passed to a brother or some other branch of the family. In 1844, Colonel Charles Kemeys-Tynte, a distant relative, sought to revive the barony. He discovered that the Middlesex coroners had made so many mistakes when they drew up the proclamation outlawing Wharton that it did not appear in the record of proclamations – indeed, it seems that no writ had ever been issued. The matter remained unresolved until 1916. A writ of summons was issued by George V and Kemeys-Tynte's son took his seat in the House of Lords.

LAW'S A LOTTERY

One of the niceties of the Commonwealth is that plaintiffs in distant lands still have the right of appeal to the Judicial Committee of the Privy Council. In 1931, a case was brought from Trinidad, then still a colony. It concerned a local lottery that was decided by spinning four discs in row, each bearing the numbers zero to nine. When the winning number 9351 came up, it was disputed by the holder of ticket number 1539, who asserted that the numbers should be read off in the usual way from left to right, not right to left the way the lottery organisers had read them. The Supreme Court of Trinidad and Tobago agreed with him, but its decision was reversed by the Privy Council on the grounds that the lottery tickets carried a condition obliging all ticket holders to abide by the decision of the stewards of the club organising it.

Illustrations

279

Plan of the City of Londo

Published by J.